Detox
Your Spiritual Life
in 40 Days

Also by Peter Graystone and published by Canterbury Press:

Signs of the Times:
The Secret Lives of Twelve Everyday Icons

A fascinating and extremely accessible read.

Third Way

The facts are fascinating and the writing is funny.
As your starter for ten, it's entertaining, informative and
thought-provoking.

Surefish.co.uk

This is a great little book and lots of fun to read. It will
open your eyes to a number of things going on around
you that you may not have been aware of before.

Baptist Times

Detox
Your Spiritual Life
in 40 Days

Peter Graystone

CANTERBURY
PRESS
Norwich

First published in 2004 by the Canterbury Press,
Norwich (a publishing imprint of Hymns Ancient &
Modern Limited, a registered charity)
St Mary's Works, St Mary's Plain,
Norwich, Norfolk, NR3 3BH

www.scm-canterburypress.co.uk

British Library Cataloguing in Publication data

A catalogue record for this book is available
from the British Library

ISBN 1-85311-606-8

Typeset by Regent Typesetting, London
Printed and bound by
Bookmarque, Croydon

For Andy and Abby
who will make the world
a better place

Contents

Detox your past

Detox your expectations

Detox your relationships

Detox your spiritual life

CONTENTS

Foreword

When Peter begins a story I am never sure where it is leading. Having worked together on the leadership team of Emmanuel Church, South Croydon, I have heard plenty of them! Sometimes they lead towards a roar of laughter. Sometimes they lead towards an insight into the ways of God that is a complete surprise. But his best stories lead towards both.

Ahead of you there are 40 days and 40 stories. I have no doubt at all that at the end of them you will feel your Christian life is in better health. But, typically of Peter, you won't just have thought about your religious life – the way you pray or worship or serve God. Instead you will be thinking about how God can shape and fulfil every part of your life – the way you work, make friends, or relax. It is how to be a Christian from Monday to Saturday that fascinates Peter; Sunday has always been a bonus!

I am setting out on this detox at the same time as you. It is quite possible that God will have changed me a lot in 40 days' time. But whatever happens, I know it will be an entertaining journey.

Rupert Higgins
Formerly vicar of
Emmanuel Church,
South Croydon

Introduction

How are you?

I presume that, like me, you have asked that question a thousand times. And I presume that, like me, you are always dreading that the person might actually tell you! Someone telling you the truth about how they feel can trap you in a corner for 40 minutes. And that would be an edited version – the whole truth might take 40 hours!

Fortunately, when you use this book it is not me to whom you will talk about your life. It is God. He has infinite patience to listen to you as you reflect on the state of your health – physical, emotional and, above all, spiritual. So take a risk and be honest with him about everything that would be too dull, difficult or dangerous to tell anyone else. And do it for 40 days!

The period of 40 days has often been seen by Christians as a suitable length of time for serious thought. Jesus spent 40 days in the desert preparing for the part of his life about which we read in the Gospels. After his resurrection he appeared to his disciples for 40 days, preparing them for the moment that would turn his mission from a little, local movement into worldwide good news. So choose 40 consecutive days and treat them as a preparation for a new turning on the path that you and God are treading side by side.

You might choose Lent, the period leading up to Easter, which Christians have traditionally used for this purpose. Alternatively, it is more or less 40 days between Christmas and the end of January – always a good time to resolve to make changes. Or the daily chapters are short and light enough to make this a summertime read instead.

The book follows the pattern of a detox. This is a technique that uses a combination of eating simple and nutritious food, exercising and relaxing in order to clean and rejuvenate the body. It gives the body a chance, over a short or long period, to expel some of the toxins that we ingest and inhale because we live in an industrialized society in the twenty-first century. Detoxing is a rigorous pursuit, but it leaves people feeling less stressed, more alert and more alive.

This detox is similar, but it will take you into areas of your life that the scores of secular books on the subject dare not explore. It will give you a chance to clean and rehabilitate your relationship with God in every way – not just your body, but your soul and spirit too. I hope that you can get rid of the spiritual toxins – unwanted habits, memories, temptations and distractions – that pollute your enjoyment of living as a follower of God. I am planning to go into rehab with you for the next few weeks, so you can compare your experiences with mine. And we will be accompanied by the writers of the Bible and inspiring Christians from history, who will be sharing their timeless wisdom with us. There will be practical ideas and prayers as well, so the detox will be thorough and will hopefully develop some lifelong healthy habits. I am praying that together we will be liberated to enjoy the life that Jesus came to give us in all its fullness.

So get ready to be restored and revitalized in your Christian life. I will ask, 'How are you?' again at the end of this 40-day detox. I do hope the answer will be, 'Overflowing with energy to praise God!'

Detox your body

Day 1

Eat well

Last autumn I found myself in conversation with a friend who is a Muslim. We were sharing a train journey during Ramadan, the month during which Muslims observe a strict fast between sunrise and sunset. Half way to our destination the train came to a standstill, so the journey was longer than we expected. I was fidgety, hungry and longing for a cup of coffee; she was completely tranquil. There are some questions one can only ask in circumstances such as these, so I found out some things I had always wanted to know. During Ramadan do young children go without food as well as adults? Is the day paced differently to compensate? Are the rules in the northern hemisphere (where days are getting shorter) different from those in the south? Do people who live in areas where the community is already poor and hungry resent an additional burden?

> They said to Jesus, 'John's disciples often fast and pray, and so do the disciples of the Pharisees, but yours go on eating and drinking.' Jesus answered, 'Can you make the guests of the bridegroom fast while he is with them? But the time will come when the bridegroom will be taken from them; in those days they will fast.'
>
> *Luke 5.33–35*

It was the answer to the last question that took me most by surprise. 'It is those who have least who value

3

Ramadan most,' my friend told me, 'because during the fast rich people know what it feels like to be poor.'

Suddenly I saw Ramadan in a new light. There are discoveries to be made during it that seem too good to be owned by Islam alone. I heard myself saying, 'Christians don't have anything which compares with that.' But I suppose we do!

Traditionally Christians have marked the weeks before Easter with fasting, self-discipline, and denying oneself casual luxuries. Lent lasts 40 days (not counting Sundays), the same length of time Jesus spent fasting in the desert that is now southern Israel in preparation for the most significant phase of the work God had called him to do.

I have to confess that I have grown up with the attitude that this kind of self-denial is unnecessary – or at least that a particular period of the year for a disciplined way of life is not needed, because that kind of behaviour should be a feature of Christian life every day. In fact, to my shame, I remember lecturing a school friend who had given up chocolate for Lent about how unhelpful such superstitions were. I don't plan to make that mistake again!

In fact, Lent as we know it is not as ancient as it seems. In the years immediately after the resurrection of Jesus, his followers used to observe a strict fast, without food or drink

> Whether you eat or drink or whatever you do, do it all for the glory of God.
>
> 1 Corinthians 10.31

of any kind, from Good Friday until dawn on Easter Sunday. They were recalling the words of Jesus who, when accused of feasting when he should have been fasting, told his followers, 'The time will come when the bridegroom will be taken from you; in those days you will fast.' Time went by, those who had known Jesus personally died, and Christians became more relaxed about the fervour with which they observed holy days. In the fifth century, church leaders were keen to establish a more focused time of devotion in preparation for Easter. The churches of different countries used different ideas to make that part of the year distinctive. It was not until 900 years after Jesus died that there was international agreement that a season of penitence should begin on Ash Wednesday, lasting just over six weeks, during which Christians had a chance to reflect on their lives and seek God's forgiveness for all they wanted to be rid of. It was (as this book is) a chance to go through a spiritual detox. A disciplined attitude to eating and drinking was regarded as essential to that process. It took a very short time for the Christian population to discover for themselves the joy of using up all the forbidden foods of Lent in one big, now-or-never party on the day before, Shrove Tuesday.

> To fast is to learn to love and appreciate food, and one's own good fortune in having it.
>
> Monica Furlong, writer, born 1930

Only those who speak English know the season as Lent. In France it is *Carême* and in Italy *Quaresima* – both of which are based on the Latin word for forty. Our word Lent is from the Anglo-Saxon word for 'lengthen' or 'swell'. That is, of course, precisely what the hours of daylight are doing at this time of year, by about five minutes each day.

By the time our train reached the station evening was closing in, and my friend and I found an Indian restaurant close by. Looking at the *dal* dish on our table, I suddenly wondered whether the lentils that are one of my favourite foods share a meaning with Lent. In fact, I subsequently discovered, they do not. But *dal*, the word used for lentils in Indian languages, is full of meaning. It means 'utterly pulverized', which is what happens to the lentils to make them into the curry that is a highlight of an Indian meal.

It cannot be a coincidence that when the poorest people of India chose a name for themselves to replace 'untouchables', to which so much stigma was attached, they chose to be known as dalits. They are part of a caste system which means that people who are born into poverty find it very difficult to escape. So dalit people get the worst jobs, like cleaning sewers by hand, and are paid the least money. Poor, scorned, and with limited access to education and health care, it is easy to understand why they would describe themselves as utterly pulverized.

> Do not limit the benefit of fasting merely to abstinence from food, for a true fast means abstaining from evil. You do not eat meat, but you gobble up your brother. Loose every unjust bond, put away resentment against your neighbours, forgive them their offences.
>
> *Ambrose, Bishop of Milan, 340–97*

I am planning to eat carefully for the next 40 days. I may even try not to eat between sunrise and sundown on a couple of the days. And I plan to eat some simple foods, like lentils (which will not be a hardship because they are delicious). I am going to do it so that the dalit people of India stay in my mind. So that, as a relatively rich person, I am reminded of those who are poor – just as some of my friends do during Ramadan.

May I suggest that you try thinking about how you eat for the next 40 days? Don't think of it as eating less; think of it as eating well.

Detox: Try to recall everything you have eaten during the past week – the meals, the snacks, the treats. Think about the speed, the company, the nourishment, and the habits you have got into. Is God trying to tell you anything about your life through your attitude to food?

God of my life, as the days swell, so may my heart. Help me to appreciate every moment, every mouthful, every meeting. Amen.

Day 2

Have a health check

No one pays much attention to the fact that the writers of the letters in the New Testament were very concerned for the physical health of the people to whom they were writing, as well as their spiritual health. Paul gave some very practical advice to his young protégé Timothy. Knowing that the purity of the water supply in Ephesus was unreliable, he recommended that his friend kept himself pure by drinking 'a little wine because of your stomach and your frequent illnesses'. It is not the same advice that we might give to someone who had just got underway on a detox, but it had the same purpose! He had previously reminded Timothy of the value of exercise, before adding that it is more important to work out spiritually than physically, because this has an impact on 'both the present life and the life to come'.

When John prayed that his friend Gaius would have a body that was as healthy as his soul, it was in contrast to the philosophy of the ancient Greeks. They assumed the body to be an evil thing, trapping the all-important soul until it is released from its prison by death. But Christians have always viewed God's creation, particularly the human body, as full of goodness. Paul calls our bodies 'temples of the Holy Spirit'.

> [My dear friend Gaius], I pray that you may enjoy good health and that all may go well with you, even as your soul is getting along well.
>
> 3 John 1.2

There could hardly be a bigger contrast than between a prison and a temple. Honourable behaviour is required in a temple, and that should have an impact on the way we treat our muscle and bone. A godless view of the body sees it merely as a vehicle for reproducing more life through as much sex as possible. A Christian view of the body sees it as something to cherish.

Jesus dignified the human body wonderfully by choosing to inhabit one when he walked and talked on our planet. That has implications for the most basic activities of our lives. It means that sex is more than just an animal urge, but something to be enjoyed imaginatively and passionately in a unique relationship of love. It means that eating and drinking are more than cravings to pour salt and fat and sugar down our throats, but are activities that can sustain our bodies in a balanced way. It means that exercise and relaxation are more than leisure pursuits, but are methods that God has given us to be comfortable inside our own skin.

> Do you not know that your bodies are temples of the Holy Spirit, who is in you, whom you have received from God? You are not your own; you were bought at a price. Therefore honour God with your bodies.
>
> I Corinthians 6.19–20

This 40 day detox begins with your body because if you feel fitter and more energetic because of the attention you are paying to your physical circumstances you will be in a much better position to make life-enhancing changes to your spiritual circumstances. How do you know that your body needs a detox? Some of the tell-tale signs are blotchy skin, swollen eyes, breath that doesn't smell fresh, unexplained mood swings, an uncomfortable neck or aching muscles, too many trivial, sniffly illnesses and an irregular digestive system. Severe instances of any of those, of course, need the advice of a doctor. But minor, irritable instances may simply be symptoms of treating your body like a prison, not a temple.

The writer of the Proverbs in the Old Testament recommended that the way to achieve health is to look to age-old wisdom that served previous generations well. 'When I was a boy,' he wrote, 'in my father's house, still tender, and an only child of my mother, he taught me and said, "Lay hold of my words with all your heart . . . for they are life to those who find them and health to a person's whole body"' (4.3, 4, 22). This is in the same spirit as the advice of those who write in health magazines today about the impact of toxins on our well-being. They point to the fact that industrial chemicals are stronger, food is more highly refined and pollution levels are higher than they were 50 years ago. Sometimes they send us back to the ways of our grandparents' generation for solutions. By doing this, the self-healing and self-cleansing techniques that God has designed as part of the way he created our bodies will have an opportunity to work as he meant them to before the amount of toxins we inhale and ingest become too much for our systems to deal with.

> Be careful to preserve your health. It is a trick of the devil, which he employs to deceive good souls, to incite them to do more than they are able, in order that they may no longer be able to do anything.
>
> Vincent de Paul, philanthropist, 1580–1660

The piece of grandmotherly advice that all experts agree on is that we should drink more water. Choose it as an alternative to sugary drinks or coffee. Refined sugar and caffeine both enter the bloodstream very quickly and have, in their own ways, negative or addictive impacts, so they are best regarded as treats rather than necessities that get you through the day. Experts also recommend choosing wholemeal bread instead of white. The scientific reason for this is that the refining process steals valuable nutrients from the grains, but grandmotherly wisdom would add that it steals most of the flavour as well. The same logic applies to other foods that are naturally good for us – fresh fruit and vegetables, fish, unsalted nuts and seeds, food that has been cooked by steaming or grilling rather than frying.

However, nutritionists set their recommendations

> Look to your health and, if you have it, praise God and value it next to a good conscience. For health is the second blessing that we mortals are capable of – a blessing that money cannot buy. Therefore value it and be thankful for it.
>
> *Izaak Walton, writer, 1593–1683*

about eating in the context of advice about taking the active option wherever there is a choice (such as using the stairs instead of a lift, and walking rather than using a car for short distances), countering stress with times of dedicated relaxation, talking openly to friends, and making sure that your work is interrupted by proper breaks and fresh air. This holistic attitude that brings together body, mind and emotions is entirely in keeping with the ancient advice in Proverbs that you should 'above all else, guard your heart, for it is the wellspring of life' (4.23). It seems to have done the world of good for Timothy, Gaius and my grandmother, so I'm ready to give it a go!

Detox: Bring to mind things that have been nagging you about your physical health, and set a target of doing something about them by the end of this 40 day detox. Make an appointment to see a doctor if necessary. Organize some exercise and stretching. Relax and breathe deeply. Book a neck and shoulder massage at a reputable health centre. Replace some or all of the caffeine and alcohol you drink with plenty of water. Get some fresh air, particularly if work or parenting require you to be in an office or at home for long periods.

Lord Jesus, when you chose to become a human being you gave such dignity to the body. Show me how to treat my body with the respect it needs and deserves. Amen.

Day 3

Recover

Of all the characters in the Bible, the one with whom I identify least is Elijah. There were times in his life when he was responsible for jaw-dropping acts of witness on behalf of God, opposing evil with great courage. Frankly, heroism is not my style. When people are doing desperately brave things I am the one who offers to bring everyone a nice cup of tea and a biscuit to keep their spirits up. I'm not so much Superman as Supperman!

However, having triumphed for God, Elijah was also susceptible to depression. I understand how people who have experienced high points in their spiritual life can then feel very low when they return to the jog-trot of life. But, to be honest, I'm not very prone to getting depressed either. I seem to be able to enjoy life without highs and lows.

Nine centuries before Jesus, Elijah had a ghastly run-in with the priests of a pagan religion in which God proved himself to be a God who answers prayer – fire blazed, rain torrented and blood flowed. Elijah emerged as God's champion, but that made him

> A great and powerful wind tore the mountains apart and shattered the rocks before the Lord, but the Lord was not in the wind. After the wind there was an earthquake, but the Lord was not in the earthquake. After the earthquake came a fire, but the Lord was not in the fire. And after the fire came a gentle whisper.
>
> *I Kings 19.11–12*

13

enemies in high places, notably Jezebel the queen. She made a blood-chilling threat to have him assassinated. Understandably Elijah was terrified. God's solution was something so straightforward that it comes as a surprise to us. He recommended, 'Run for it!' So Elijah did!

As Christians, we do not have to face every situation like a cartoon superhero. Obviously there are some circumstances in which we need to take a stand against something that is wrong. But there are other occasions when it is fine for a Christian to admit defeat and make an exit – times when stress has reduced our capacity to be useful for God, or times when so much has been asked of us that it has taken a physical or emotional toll. God doesn't call us to be successful in everything we do; he calls us to be obedient in everything we do.

That is why it is so important to detox your spiritual life. And although Elijah could never have understood the concept, it is curious to notice the length of time it took for God to repair his weary body and soul – 40 days!

> What do people get for all the toil and anxious striving with which they labour under the sun? All their days their work is pain and grief; even at night their minds do not rest. This too is meaningless. People can do nothing better than to eat and drink and find satisfaction in their work. This too, I see, is from the hand of God, for without him who can eat or find enjoyment?
>
> *Ecclesiastes 2.22–25*

After the triumph, the terror and the running away, Elijah was left exhausted and alone. The Bible's account tells us: 'He came to a broom tree, sat down under it and prayed that he might die. "I have had enough, Lord," he said.' Did God diagnose that Elijah had a deep spiritual problem that required the casting out of evil and hours of prayer? No, he did not! He provided just what your grandmother would recommend: rest, food and company. The story goes on: 'He lay down under the tree and fell asleep. All at once an angel touched him and said, "Get up and eat." He looked around, and there by his head was a cake of bread and a jar of water. He ate and drank, and then went back to sleep again.' Never overlook the value of the ordinary gifts of God in a rush to find a spiritual response to your need. That is why the detox you have begun needs to address some basic issues of nutrition and health as part of examining your relationship with God.

But Elijah needed something extra in order to recover from the sense of failure that had enveloped him. He felt he had not lived up to the expectations his ancestors had of him, and that he did not deserve what had happened: 'I have been very zealous for the Lord God. I am the only one left, and now they are trying to kill me too.'

> It is true that the voice of God, having once fully penetrated the heart, becomes strong as a tempest and louder than thunder; but before reaching the heart it is as weak as a light breath which scarcely agitates the air. It shrinks from noise, and is silent amid agitation.
>
> *Ignatius of Loyola, founder of the Jesuits, 1491–1556*

God's response was to take Elijah back to the roots of where his trust and faith began. Mount Horeb was the place where God had revealed himself to the Hebrew people and started a loving relationship with them. It was there that Elijah rediscovered the presence of God. It didn't come in the way he expected. Nothing like it! There was a storm, but God wasn't there. Nine hundred years later there would be a storm on Lake Galilee which Jesus calmed, and God would speak mightily through that. But not this time! There was an earthquake, but God wasn't there. Nine hundred years later there would be an earth-quake at the time of Jesus' resurrection, and God would speak triumphantly through that. But not this time! There was fire, but God wasn't there. Nine hundred years later the Holy Spirit would come in tongues of fire, and God would speak through that in a way which changed the world for all time. But not this time!

Instead there was a gentle whisper! That is the sort of touch of God on our lives that we might completely miss. But it is certainly true that one of the things we can do when we feel exhausted spiritually is to retrace our steps to the point where God first began to be real in our lives. Where did God first take us by surprise? During this detox it is unlikely that he will make himself known in dramatic ways. But a quiet whisper – unspectacular, ordinary – might turn out to be just what we need.

> Watch, dear Lord, with those who wake or watch or weep tonight, and give your angels charge over those who sleep. O Lord Christ, rest your weary ones.
>
> *Augustine, Bishop of Hippo, 354–430*

That is the ordinary way God comes alongside us. It is not sensational, but it is genuine, and it can start a recovery in our lives. As a Christian you are not alone. A still, small voice! You are not alone, you are not alone, you are not alone!

Detox: Look in your diary at your plans for the fortnight ahead. When will be the highly-charged days? And, within those days, which will be the most stressful hours? Reserve time after those events in which to recover, with nourishing food, rest and the kind of company you enjoy. Plan your recovery and write it in your diary now.

Lord God, I don't need anything dramatic; I just need something reassuring. Whisper to me that I am not alone. Amen.

Day 4

Get some sleep

If you were the president of the most powerful country in the world for 24 hours, what would you do? James Polk was President of the USA for four years and stood down from office at noon on Sunday, 4 March 1849. His successor, Zachary Taylor, was an extremely pious Christian and refused to be sworn in on a Sunday, so he did not begin his presidency until the next day. Under normal circumstances the vice-president would have held the office for the intervening period, but George Dallas had resigned the previous week. So, for one day only, the presidency was held by a man whose name has been long forgotten – the senior senator, David Rice Atchison. And why has his name not entered the history books? Because he was so exhausted from making arrangements for the inauguration that he arrived home in the early hours of the morning, went to bed, and slept through his entire day in office.

The reason I warm towards Senator Atchison is that when he talked about it afterwards he didn't speak as if it were a wasted opportunity, but as the most sensible thing to do in the circumstances. We usually think about sleep as an absence of activity. It seems like a negative but necessary activity to recover from the positive but tiring events of the day. What would happen if, for a short while, we made sleep one of the priorities of our lives and built the rest of the day around it?

We have Jesus' example to follow. Crowds kept him up late and woke him up early. He seems to have made a decision not to keep going until he was burnt out, but to stop whenever he knew he needed to. Mark's Gospel tells us that at one point, after an exhausting time of teaching about the Kingdom of God, Jesus abandoned the crowd (that is the literal translation) and got in a boat 'just as he was'. And so, either extremely exhausted or extremely confident, Jesus was able to sleep through a squall. When he was woken up by his disciples he was angry. I presume it was because they did not trust him to rescue them, but it is tempting to think that he was cross with them for rousing him from the depths of his sleep! Either way, it is interesting to see the contrast between Jesus' reactions and those of his disciples. They saw the sea unsettled and assumed that the best response was to become as restless as nature was. But Jesus' response was to put the storm to sleep, just as he had been. Both responses would have ended up with humans at one with nature, but Jesus' actions lend great dignity to sleep as something God-given – a blessing of creation. Sleep isn't laziness; it's holiness!

> Leaving the crowd behind, [Jesus' disciples] took him along, just as he was, in the boat. There were also other boats with him. A furious squall came up, and the waves broke over the boat, so that it was nearly swamped. Jesus was in the stern, sleeping on a cushion. The disciples woke him and said to him, 'Teacher, don't you care if we drown?' He got up, rebuked the wind and said to the waves, 'Quiet! Be still!' Then the wind died down and it was completely calm. He said to his disciples, 'Why are you so afraid? Do you still have no faith?'
>
> *Mark 4.36–40*

Of course, the Bible is not so affirming about sleep that it becomes an excuse for being indolent. The Proverbs of the

Old Testament warn us that idleness is a route to ruin: 'How long will you lie there, you sluggard? When will you get up from your sleep? A little sleep, a little slumber, a little folding of the hands to rest – and poverty will come on you like a bandit' (6.9–11). So how can we tell whether an extra hour or two in bed is a valuable part of a spiritual detox or just giving in to lethargy? Once again, Proverbs is helpful, because it encourages us to train ourselves to know our bodies and read the signs they give so that we can judge what they are telling us we need: 'My son, preserve sound judgment and discernment, do not let them out of your sight; they will be life for you . . . when you lie down, you will not be afraid; when you lie down, your sleep will be sweet' (3.21–24).

The fact is that this generation is offered far more alternatives to going to bed than any previous one. After the sun went down for Jesus' generation the possibilities were limited – lighting a room artificially was expensive and complicated, which thus increased the appeal of two things for which the dark is suited, one of which is sleep! However, electric light at the flick of a switch, television through the night, and an internet that (like God himself) will neither slumber nor sleep, have created endless alternatives. The result is that children at the beginning of the twenty-first century are having an average of two hours sleep per day less than their grandparents did at the same stage of their lives.

> In vain you rise early and stay up late, toiling for food to eat – for God grants sleep to those he loves.
>
> *Psalm 127.2*

Researchers are understandably concerned about the physical and mental toll of this, and recommend that we all take the simple pleasure that sleep offers far more seriously. Their advice to those who want to detox their lives of restlessness is to establish a regular sleep pattern as part of a daily routine. They suggest that we will benefit if the end of our day is occupied with activities that relax us, such as reading or having a bath. And their evidence shows that taking care over the position we choose when we get into bed can improve the quality of our sleep.

> Blessings on him who created sleep, the mantle that covers all human thoughts, the food that satisfies hunger, the drink that slakes thirst, the fire that warms cold, the cold that moderates heat, the common currency that buys all things, the balance that equalises the shepherd and the king, the simpleton and the sage.
>
> *Cervantes, author of* Don Quixote, *1547–1616*

> Those who have the gale of the Holy Spirit advance even when they are asleep.
>
> *Brother Lawrence, monk, 1611–91*

They recommend being conscious of having our spines in a straight line whether we sleep on our backs or sides, and suggest that we have one good quality pillow, and lie on it so that our necks are not pulled in awkward angles.

Treat sleep as a gift that God has given us because he loves us. Perhaps for 40 days the third of the day that is wasted could become the third of the day during which God does something wonderful for us.

Detox: For the next few days, write down the hours that you intend to sleep in your diary, as if your sleep is an appointment that you intend to prioritize. Fit in your other activities around it, and monitor whether you feel more refreshed as your body gets used to the discipline.

Lord God, before I am exhausted from filling every last second, earning every last penny, pushing every last boundary, show me a better way. Amen.

Day 5

Shake yourself awake

Today's detox follows yesterday's as surely as day follows night!

'Why are you sleeping?' The question gets asked twice in the Gospels. Jesus asks it of his disciples at the worst moment of their lives in the Garden of Gethsemane, with the collapse of their mission staring them in the face. The disciples ask it of Jesus at the scariest moment of their lives, on a boat in the middle of a storm.

Sleep gets mixed reviews in the Bible. Its first appearance, in the myths of the Garden of Eden, is glorious. Adam goes into a deep sleep and, while he is oblivious to anything, God forms womankind. When he wakes up, there she is: his soulmate, his helpmate; his equal, his opposite; his love and his lust. Eve! And suddenly there is a good reason not to sleep at night!

That, according to the Bible, was in the glorious days before sin entered the world. After that sleep is sometimes easy and sometimes impossible. It is sometimes blessed with dreams and sometimes cursed with

> The hour has come for you to wake up from your slumber, because our salvation is nearer now than when we first believed. The night is nearly over; the day is almost here. So let us put aside the deeds of darkness and put on the armour of light. Let us behave decently, as in the daytime.
>
> *Romans 13.11–13*

nightmares. Sometimes it soothes away cares and sometimes it's disturbing.

Dreadful things happen while people are asleep. Noah gets so drunk that in his sleep he doesn't realize he has no clothes on, which unleashes a train of ghastly events. Samson is so shagged out after his night with the prostitute Delilah that he is captured by the Philistines, instigating a series of atrocities. Eutychus is so bored listening to a long sermon that he drops off, both into sleep and out of a third storey window.

This puts me in a difficult position, because I love sleep. The night in October when we get an extra hour is one of my autumn highlights. Aged eight on our school trip to the pantomime *Sleeping Beauty*, all the good boys came out wanting to be the sword-swishing hero. All the bad boys wanted to be the blood-curdling ogre. I wanted to be the princess who slept for a hundred years!

So I am gritting my teeth as I admit that whenever sleep is used as a metaphor in the New Testament it is bad news. 'Wake up!' the writers tell us repeatedly. Things are going wrong in the world and you are sleepwalking through it. 'Wake up!' because Jesus is going to return any moment. There is so much to do and so little time. Apathy, temptation, lack of energy to copy the ways of Jesus, being a Christian by name but not showing evidence of it – the New Testament writers describe these things as being asleep

> It is shameful even to mention what the disobedient do in secret. But everything exposed by the light becomes visible, for it is light that makes everything visible. This is why it is said: 'Wake up, O sleeper, rise from the dead, and Christ will shine on you.' Be very careful, then, how you live – not as unwise but as wise, making the most of every opportunity.
>
> *Ephesians 5.12–16*

while the night deepens into danger. Not the best metaphor they could have chosen for someone like me!

But it was Jesus himself who started the metaphor. In Gethsemane he had to wake his followers physically; in his teaching he had to wake them spiritually. He once told a story about a disastrous wedding celebration. At a wedding in Jesus' day, the bride's family prepared her intricate costume and then sat down to wait for the groom's arrival. (It was the opposite of today's weddings where the stereotypical joke is that the bride keeps the groom waiting.) In the meantime, everyone dozed off. When a rap on the door woke them all up, half the bridesmaids were ready to go to the party, but half discovered that they did not have what they needed for the wedding procession and were subsequently left behind. The problem was not that they had needed a sleep; it was that they had wasted time while they were awake and had failed to get themselves ready.

> Life is a hard fight, a struggle, a wrestling . . . The night is given to us to take breath, to pray, to drink deep at the fountain of power. The day, to use the strength which has been given us, to go forth and work with it till the evening.
> *Florence Nightingale, nurse, 1820–1910*

'Be prepared for my arrival,' says Jesus the bridegroom. How? By doing as a habit what we want him to see us doing when he arrives in person. Being wide awake!

The Christian faith is not a matter of dozing our way through Monday to Saturday before snapping into religious mode on a Sunday. It is a matter of having our relationship with Jesus in mind, shaping and prompting us, all through the week. It is when we are drowsy (either actually or metaphorically) that we allow things to happen that we regret when we are awake. Be alert, Jesus says, not only when you know I am close, but during the gaps when it is harder to be aware of me. Even then, I am on the way!

I am on the way! The challenge comes blazingly from Paul in the New Testament: 'The hour has come for you to wake up from your slumber.' It comes perfectly from Jesus in Luke's Gospel: 'Get up and pray so that you will not fall into temptation.' And it comes pathetically from a writer who at eight o'clock in the morning would give anything in the world to press the snooze button one more time, but who believes with all his heart that the world needs Jesus to prevent it from sleepwalking into chaos.

> Be eager in prayer, and vigilant to do good without wearying. Remove from yourself all drowsiness. You should be watchful both by night and day. Do not be disheartened.
>
> *Abraham of Nathpar, theologian, circa 550–600*

The challenge to the Christians of the world is for all the dozers to perk up, all the deserters to join up, all the idlers to hurry up, all the loungers to sit up, all the miseries to cheer up, all the bores to shut up, all the whisperers to speak up and, most of all, for all the sleepers to wake up, because it was while the disciples were sleeping that Jesus was betrayed.

Detox: Where are the places and when are the times that you are most likely to fail the standards that Jesus has set you? Last thing at night? After a drink? In a particular shop? With certain people? As part of your detox, analyse whether there are areas of your life in which you need to be shaken awake, and take steps to make sure you do not let your guard down.

Lord Jesus, you and I both know the circumstances in which I am most likely to let you down. Make me strong enough not to go where I will be tempted, and make me vigilant when I have no choice. Amen.

Day 6

Change pace

Let's hear it for the ai! This magnificent creature, which is also known as the three-toed sloth, is not only a lifesaver in the closing stages of a game of Scrabble, but is indisputably the most lethargic mammal in God's creation. It spends much of its life upside down in a Brazilian tree, where it passes about 20 hours per day dozing. It has a peaceful, vegetarian life completely in harmony with its environment. Fully motivated the ai can reach a maximum speed of 250 metres per hour – 400 times slower than a jaguar. But that is in an emergency. The speed at which it likes to travel is about five metres per hour. It is the laziest living thing that ever boasted a backbone.

However, going through life at such a slow pace doesn't seem to do the ai any harm. In fact the reverse! The sloth is one of the most successful mammals in evolutionary history. At such a slow pace it evades the attention of

> We know that in all things God works for the good of those who love him, who have been called according to his purpose. For those God foreknew he also predestined to be conformed to the likeness of his Son, that he might be the firstborn among many brothers and sisters. And those he predestined, he also called; those he called, he also justified; those he justified, he also glorified. What, then, shall we say in response to this? If God is for us, who can be against us?
>
> Romans 8.28–31

all its natural predators and triumphs over jaguars and eagles with a serene smile.

I am the reverse. That's my problem! I need everything to happen now. I never want to be reading a book; I want to have read a book! It is no good telling me that everything will be all right in the end; I want it all to be right now! I want poverty to end today. I want men of violence to put down their weapons this instant. It is agony having to wait patiently for God to act. He is making his way through the whole of eternity to bring about his plan for humankind, but I only have a few moments between birth and death to be human. I am speeding through life like a jaguar, and God is working out his plan like an ai. Just as the jaguar moves so fast that he doesn't even see the sloth edging onwards, so we operate at such speed that we miss God's relentless progress towards an utter triumph.

> Christ Jesus, who died – more than that, who was raised to life – is at the right hand of God and is also interceding for us. Who shall separate us from the love of Christ? Shall trouble or hardship or persecution or famine or nakedness or danger or sword? . . . No, in all these things we are more than conquerors through him who loved us.
>
> *Romans 8.34–37*

The creator of the world is greater than anything he created and will rise to defeat all that challenges his goodness. It is a truth that is easy to accept on lazy, sunny days; harder to hang on to in times of darkness and injustice. But the message of the Bible is that we are destined to share in God's triumph, and that the bad things which distract us are merely part of a plan that is unshakeably good. Saint Paul put it like this: 'In all things God works for the good of those who love him.'

Paul uses four key words to describe what God is doing. 'Predestined' tells us that the relationship we have with God is outside time altogether. Forever has he known what his good plan is for humankind, and forever has he been able to see the unimaginable future in which we will be with him. 'Called' speaks of what God has done in our past, taking an astonishing initiative to invite us to be with him on his progress towards victory. 'Justified' tells us where we are at present. It means being accepted by God, with our sins forgiven and our friendship with him restored, all because of what Jesus has done on our behalf. 'Glorified' points to the place where we shall be in the future, alongside God and sharing the justice, joy and peace of a perfect heaven.

Future, present, past and an eternity outside time altogether. That's the timescale God is working on. No wonder we can't keep up with him. It's not because we can't go fast enough; it's because we can't go slow enough. In this life we will never be able to. It is only in death that we will finally slow down to God's own pace and understand perfectly.

> God walks slowly because he is love. If he is not love he would have gone much faster. Love has its speed. It is an inner speed. It is a spiritual speed. It is a different kind of speed from the technological speed to which we are accustomed . . . It goes on in the depth of our life, whether we notice it or not, whether we are currently hit by a storm or not, at three miles per hour. It is the speed we walk, and therefore it is the speed the love of God walks.
>
> Kosuke Koyama, theologian, born 1929

Nothing, least of all death, will be able to separate us from God's love. How? 'Through him who loved us.' It is all down to Jesus. Obviously we are not good enough; but Jesus is good enough. Obviously we are not powerful enough; but Jesus is infinitely strong. Obviously the mess we get ourselves into is anything but triumphant; but Jesus has already triumphed. When you put yourself on Jesus' side, you are putting yourself on the side of love and goodness. You are putting yourself on the winning side. Unstoppable!

> The mills of God grind slowly, but they grind exceeding small.
>
> Friedrich von Logau, poet, 1604–55

Sadness, hunger, poverty, war – we see these things all too readily, and it is understandable that we lose sight of the loving God who, on a different timescale from ours, has all these things in his grip. Living at a pace which allows you to see him at work requires practice. It involves allowing God to refocus your eyes from our human timescale to the eternity in which he is working to put right all that humans have put wrong. Practise living in the love of Jesus, the love from which nothing can separate you now and for all eternity, and get ready for all things to be swept up in the inevitable triumph of good.

Detox: Set aside an hour this week to go at a different pace. (A whole day would be better, but an hour is more realistic.) Go through it slowly and relish every moment. Eat some food and taste it properly. Take a bath and enjoy it to the full. Notice colours. Go at the speed of a three-toed sloth. If you meet anyone you know, smile serenely as if you're in the Brazilian rain forest, and hang around. Dwell on all that God has done. If there are troubles in your mind, stop and pray about them. Slowly get ready for eternity.

Lord God, until I am sure enough to trust, until I am quiet enough to listen, until I am still enough to understand, slow me down and teach me patience. Amen.

Day 7

Break a habit

Freedom! Everyone wants it. The trouble is that someone else's freedom always seems more appealing than your own. Teenagers tell you they are longing for the day when they are liberated from school. Professionals tell you they wish they could reclaim the freedom of their schooldays. Last week somebody said to me, 'It must be wonderful for you not to have children. It makes you free to do whatever you want with your life.' I felt a searing urge to reach out my hand and enthusiastically shake the woman by the throat.

Experience has made me adept at dealing with the stupid things people say. At a wedding last summer someone I hadn't seen for 20 years said to me, 'Have you managed to find yourself a woman yet?' I was really cross, so I pretended to look forlorn and said, 'Well, to be honest, I gave up hope after the amputation.' The shock on her face as she tried to work out the politically correct response was a treat, but I

> What then? Shall we sin because we are not under law but under grace? By no means! ... When you were slaves to sin, you were free from the control of righteousness. What benefit did you reap at that time from the things you are now ashamed of? Those things result in death! But now that you have been set free from sin and have become slaves to God, the benefit you reap leads to holiness, and the result is eternal life.
>
> *Romans 6.15–22*

had to limp through the entire reception to keep up the pretence.

As Christians God has set us free. But it's an awkward freedom, because it brings with it a huge list of things one is not supposed to do. I have been involved in an exchange of e-mails with Saint Paul recently, which went like this:

Me: I feel trapped.

Saint Paul: Push off! I'm busy writing Romans.

Me: But it's urgent.

Paul: They're throwing me to the lions next week. Don't talk to me about urgent!

Me: That's just what I need to talk about. You're under arrest because you worship Jesus, but you say you're freer than you ever were before.

Paul: It's not that kind of freedom. I'm free because we have a God who is loving and merciful when we have done things wrong, and there is nothing that he enjoys more than to forgive our sins.

Me: Right then! I have a fantastic idea about freedom. Let's sin as often as we can, so that God will enjoy being loving and forgiving even more.

Paul: That is the most ridiculous thing I have ever heard!

Me: Don't disappoint me! I'm hoping for orgies on a Saturday night followed by forgiveness on a Sunday morning.

Paul: Hard luck, mate! Nice try! (We've got a right one here!) Look up what I wrote in Romans. You can find it on the internet.

In Romans, Paul explains that people who are not Christians think they can do whatever they please, but in fact they haven't got the freedom they imagine. It's as if they were slaves to sin and forced to do what God declares to be wrong. Forced to accept the world systems that keep

> You were called to be free. But do not use your freedom to indulge the sinful nature; rather, serve one another in love.
>
> *Galatians 5.13*

poor people poor while rich people get the best deal. Forced to go along with society's standards that anything is acceptable in sex as long as no one gets distressed. Forced to accept that the person who pushes their weight around is going to get their way. These things have enticing names: free market, free love, free-for-all. But there's nothing free about them; they are part of a world that is enslaved.

When you become a Christian, you don't stop being the slave and start being the boss; you stop being the slave to one thing and become a slave to another. You become God's slave. Why is that appealing? It is hard to grasp, because slavery is not a daily reality in this country as it was in Paul's day. But low-grade addiction is – to nicotine, caffeine, chocolate or any one of a thousand habits. And since Paul seems to have mastered e-mail he can probably understand tobacco as well!

> If you notice something evil in yourself, correct it. If something good, take care of it. If something beautiful, cherish it. If something sound, preserve it. If something unhealthy, heal it. Do not weary of reading the ways of the Lord, and you will be adequately instructed by them so as to know what to avoid and what to go after.
>
> *Bernard of Clairvaux, founder of the Cistercian order of monks, 1091–1153*

Saint Paul: Becoming a Christian is like breaking free from an addiction to cigarettes.

Me: I can't help it. I don't even want to do it, but I need the nicotine. I know it's smelly, my friends think it's revolting, and there's every chance I'll die from it, but it's beyond my control.

Paul: Then make a complete break. Throw away your ashtrays, get rid of your lighter, snip your leftovers in two, and never have another puff.

Me: That's not being set free; that's being imprisoned. I've lost my freedom ever to enjoy a cigarette again.

Paul: Yes. Welcome to prison! Welcome to breathing clean air. Welcome to food that tastes fabulous. Welcome to clothes that don't smell. Welcome to good health. You're going to have a new addiction now – addiction to never smoking again. You don't want to go back to old habits do you?

This illustrates what Paul meant when he wrote: 'What benefit did you reap at that time from the things you are now ashamed of? Those things result in death! But now that you have been set free from sin and have become slaves to God, the benefit you reap leads to holiness.'

As a Christian, do you miss any of the things that the rest of society seems to do without restraint? Welcome to clean air. Welcome to living without shame. Welcome to knowing that God is delighted by holiness. Welcome to life.

You don't want to go back to the way the rest of the world lives! Don't dabble with it. Make a clean break. Throw out anything that has tempting, ashen traces of wrongdoing on it. Don't go near where old habits led you. Have a new way of life. A new addiction. Addicted to good. Addicted to God.

> Be both a servant and free: a servant in that you are subject to God, but free in that you are not enslaved to anything – either to empty praise or to any of the passions.
>
> *John of Apamea, monk, circa 400–50*

Detox: Break a habit! Analyse the things you do regularly and ask whether any of them are in control of you, rather than being things you choose. Even if it is only for a specific length of time, overcome the habit to demonstrate your freedom. And thank God too for the freedom to worship him.

Lord Jesus, free me from all that holds me back in my desire to be wholly yours. Let nothing but you demand my undivided loyalty. Amen.

Detox your standards

Day 8

Open a door

Just after my fortieth birthday I did something that changed my life forever. I let a homeless teenager come and live in my home. I am sure that most families would have dealt with this by making a few well-considered adjustments. However, I had been living by myself for 16 years, so to share my house with anyone required a revolution, let alone sharing it with someone whose behaviour had become entirely unpredictable as relationships with his family deteriorated over several years.

The best way to describe the new situation is by comparing it with fireworks – both glorious and explosive! It has certainly made me a different person and, I hope, a better one. Singleness shapes some people into generous and loving maturity; others grow self-centred and crotchety in old age. I could not bear to become a self-centred person. But if you live by yourself you are simply not aware of whether you are selfish or not. You do what you do

Since, then, you have been raised with Christ, set your hearts on things above, where Christ is seated at the right hand of God. Set your minds on things above, not on earthly things. For you died, and your life is now hidden with Christ in God. When Christ, who is your life, appears, then you also will appear with him in glory. Put to death, therefore, whatever belongs to your earthly nature.

Colossians 3.1–5

without having to make reference to anyone else – the question of whether it might be seen as selfish never needs to enter your mind. But sharing your life with someone forces you to see the space around yourself quite differently.

An example! My bedroom door doesn't close. I don't know why it won't close – it never has done! It's only the last inch that doesn't shut, so when I lived by myself it didn't bother me in the slightest. Well, why would it? But as soon as Paul moved in, I could think of nothing else but that inch of open door. Not only had his *Playstation* taken over my TV, his heavy metal music taken residence in my CD player, his beer run rampant in my fridge, and his chaotic roguishness charmed its way into every part of the house that we share, but I couldn't even close my own bedroom door!

I am not sure why it irritated me so much. It's not as if I keep a stash of drugs hidden in my bedroom, or pornography on top of the wardrobe! But the one inch of my life that I could no longer keep secret really unsettled me.

So I drove to my parents to borrow a plane, but I forgot to take it away with me. I tried someone from my church, but they were on holiday, and someone else had the right tool but the wrong attachment. For one reason or another time went by and I couldn't get hold of what I needed. And an unexpected thing happened – I got used to living with the door open. Instead of changing the door, so that I could

[The Spirit says:] 'These are the words of him who is holy and true, who holds the key of David. What he opens no one can shut, and what he shuts no one can open. I know your deeds. See, I have placed before you an open door that no one can shut. I know that you have little strength, yet you have kept my word and have not denied my name.'

Revelation 3.7–8

live in the way I used to, I found that I had changed my behaviour so that it didn't matter whether the door was open or shut.

It strikes me that this is a powerful picture of how I want to lead the whole of my Christian life. I want to come to the point at which people could peep through the door at anything I do, hear anything I say, tune into anything I think, and I could display it all with complete integrity. I would not be ashamed or embarrassed, even slightly, by the difference between the standards Jesus has set me and the standards I actually keep.

Oh boy! That is what I want in theory, but there is a daunting amount that needs to be dealt with if I am ever going to live my whole life with the door open. If I am to live with God's will done on earth as it is in heaven, as I have prayed thousands of times over the years, I need a total change of attitude.

And heaven is where that change of attitude begins. If Jesus is raised from the dead, as Christians proclaim, then there is a real sense in which we who have joined ourselves to him in our Christian faith are also raised from the dead with him. Not in the future, but in the present! A person who has allied himself or herself to Christ has, in a sense, already died to what went before and is raised with Jesus to become part of the heavenly community. Jesus sees us spiritually as already with him in heaven. All we are doing is waiting for our bodies to catch up with the reality.

> Open wide the windows of our spirits and fill us full of light. Open wide the doors of our hearts, that we may receive and entertain thee with all our powers of adoration.
>
> *Christina Rossetti, poet, 1830–94*

If the fact of the matter is that our home is with God in heaven, then that ought to make a noticeable difference.

The only logical response is for our behaviour from day to day to be godly. Heavenly! If we really believe that what Jesus has done for us has opened the door between heaven and earth, then we need to live our Christian lives with the door open.

The Bible's challenge is this: Be what you are. There are things in our lives that we don't want other Christians to find out about. If it were possible, we would prefer that God didn't find out about them either. We would rather keep them hidden. They are the things for which we need a fully functional door.

So how do you know what to do when you are living with the door open? Imagine what standards will feel natural, easy, comfortable, joyful to everyone in heaven, and set your heart on living them out on earth. They won't feel so easy and probably not so gratifying from a personal point of view, but they will feel right. What standards of language will seem enriching in

> Value the silent power of a consistent life.
>
> *Florence Nightingale, nurse, 1820–1910*

heaven? Use them now with confidence and there will be nothing that you can only say behind closed doors. What sexual standards will seem selfless and thrilling in heaven? Practise them now so that there is nothing which seems a guilty secret. How will your relationships with people look in heaven, when hurts and jealousies and lies are things of the past? Live out now what you actually are: someone hidden with Christ, not someone concealing dusty stuff in a corner that the vacuum cleaner will never quite reach.

Paul, I think I'm going to take the door off its hinges!

Detox: Make a mental list of things in your life that you would rather keep hidden – not necessarily objects, but invisible things such as thoughts, habits and attitudes. Bring them one by one into God's presence and consider what he might be telling you about himself.

Lord Jesus Christ, help me to turn my home into a place of goodness, care and integrity, fit to welcome you in whenever I open the door. Amen.

Day 9

Get busy

The alarm goes off. It is 7.40 am. I have slept well. No crick in the neck, no anxiety about the day. There is time to pray to God. And there is also the snooze button.

God. Snooze button.

Snooze button. God! Zzzzzz!

What? Surely that wasn't ten minutes! Am I going to catch the train? Just about! I can pray while I'm in the shower. There's no sound from Paul's bedroom. He must have a day off. I tiptoe down the corridor, pull back the shower curtain, reach out and press the . . . bang, bang, bang!

'Peter, mate! It's an emergency. I have to be at work in 15 minutes.'

'But Paul, I'm in the shower.'

'You've been in there 20 minutes.'

'I've been in here 20 seconds!'

'Can I use the bathroom first? Please!' As I quickstep out, Paul hip-hops in. The last time you saw naked men dance this fast was in a Kylie Minogue video.

I rush breakfast. Paul reappears, gleaming. He is in black trousers and a shirt I haven't seen him wearing before. Hang on! *My shirt!* 'You don't mind, do you? I haven't got one that's ironed.'

'But now I haven't got one that's . . .'

'Bye!' The door bangs shut! Now I really am in trouble.

Where's the ironing board? Woosh. Swish. Tuck. I can *just* do this. I'm walking, fast but dignified, down the road.

A fish, going ludicrously fast, sweeps round the corner and misses me by an inch. It's a Christian fish. I can tell it's a Christian fish because it's got a car attached. I'm livid! A man leans out the window to apologize. I can't stop to listen. I'm now in serious danger of missing the train.

I will be fine as long as there's no queue at the ticket machine. I'm trembling as I press the buttons. A notice appears: 'No change. Use coins.' I only have a £20 note. There are 12 people in the queue at the ticket office. A woman is paying for a season ticket. In pennies! There are inspectors at the gateway. All I can do is throw myself on their mercy. 'Please! I have to chair a meeting at 9.00. Can I get my ticket at the other end?' The train is rumbling into the station. There are tears coming into my eyes. 'Please!'

> Whatever you do, whether in word or deed, do it all in the name of the Lord Jesus, giving thanks to God the Father through him.
>
> *Colossians 3.17*

'All right!' I could hug the man!

I scamper to the platform. I am Jonathan Edwards. I sail through the air as the doors close. I'm on the train. At the other end I race through the streets and I enter the meeting room at 8.59.

Colleagues arrive. It's an unspectacular meeting about budgets, dates and deadlines. I am just asking whether there is any other business when Dorothy gives a sigh and slumps onto the table. I don't panic. She has only fainted. I ask, 'Who is the trained first aider for this building?' The others look at each other sheepishly, and someone says, 'Dorothy is!' I decide to call an ambulance. It is 9.45. So far I have made Paul late for work, nearly caused a car crash, broken the law in order to catch a train, and sent a colleague to hospital. We haven't had coffee yet!

Each of you should use whatever gift you have received to serve others, faithfully administering God's grace in its various forms. If you speak, you should do it as those who speak the very words of God. If you serve, you should do it with the strength God provides, so that in all things God may be praised.

1 Peter 4.10–11

And God, whom I love deeply and have been meaning to pray to since the day began, has not had a look in!

I live a busy life. When I devote no special time to God I am a failure. Surely? Well, maybe not. Not all of us have a life that can accommodate solitude and quiet. Is there perhaps another way to seek God?

Don't seek God as an alternative to the busy day. Instead, seek God *through* the busyness of the day. Let the events of each ordinary day be the actual way in which God is speaking to you. Practise finding the presence of God in all the activities and relationships.

Let's rewind the clock! The alarm goes off at 7.40 am. I press the snooze button. I will never be the kind of person who gets up at the crack of dawn for time alone with God – I just haven't got that kind of constitution. I won't feel guilty about it. I have ten minutes extra in bed. Thank you God for this warmth. Thank you God for this comfort. For the hot water in the pipes. For the splendid young man who lodges in my house. May I always be aware of goodness in God's world!

The time of busyness does not differ from the time of prayer; and in the noise and clutter of my kitchen, while several people are calling for different things at the same time, I possess God in as great tranquillity as if I were upon my knees at the blessed sacrament.

Brother Lawrence, monk, 1611–91

I am confronted with someone who needs a shower and a shirt more than me. The way I react in this relationship is where my Christian faith meets the reality of daily life. These small decisions are what I am a Christian for. The times I say 'yes' and the times I say 'no', and the grace with which I do so, are how God shows me his way through a busy day. May I always be godly in trivial decisions as well as large ones!

I narrowly avoid losing my temper with someone who nearly causes a car accident. My pounding heart leaps with relief when an official lets me onto the train. How I cope with my anger, and the honesty with which I treat the money I owe the railway company, show people how I recognize Jesus in the world. May I always recognize him in unexpected places!

I am present at a business meeting which seems to be concerned with things far from the mind of God – money and management. I deal with a minor emergency. But in all these things, not just in church, I am using the gifts God has given me. May I always use them well, as if it is Jesus who needs these things done!

Train yourself to notice God in all that whizzes past you. See the orderliness of bricks in a wall, and thank God that his creation is not haphazard. Smell the rain on the pavement and be aware of the senses he has given you. Feel the ground beneath your running feet, and be aware of our rock-solid God. And when it all seems to be going wrong, ask him, 'What are you teaching me here? How will this be valuable to me in the future?' Don't let God's work loom so small in your life as to assume that he will only speak to you when you are not busy!

> Teach me, my God and King,
> In all things thee to see,
> And what I do in anything,
> To do it as for thee.
>
> *George Herbert, poet and clergyman, 1593–1633*

Detox: Make a conscious effort through this day to allow people and circumstances to remind you that God is present.

Lord God, when I need energy because of the pace of life, make me fast; when I need rest from the rush of life, hold me fast. Amen.

Day 10

Reflect God's values

Looking at an old photograph of someone you can tell instantly which decade it comes from. It amuses me that in 50 years time, people will look at photos of my friends and think, 'Hooded top, mobile phone, bottle of water, goatee beard, permanent look of being in need of a holiday. Yes! That was taken in Croydon at the turn of the century.' The way we choose to present ourselves immediately reveals where we belong.

So you drag yourself out of bed in the morning and stagger to the bathroom. You draw yourself up to as near vertical as you can manage and look in the mirror. Your hair looks as if something evil nested in it during the night. There's glue in your eyes and a trickle of drool making its way down your chin. Do you think to yourself, 'My word, I look gorgeous! That is just the kind of image of me I want to project to the world!'?

Frankly, no! The point of looking in a mirror is to find out what needs to be done by way of damage repair. You look at your reflection to find out what changes need to be made, you do something about it, and then you set off to meet the challenges of the day looking as reasonable as you can.

The letters of the New Testament were written in the hope that they would produce churches that were full of Christian people whose activities were so distinctive that it was a dead giveaway where they belonged. Or rather, a living giveaway! But those distinctive activities were rarely

49

Everyone should be quick to listen, slow to speak and slow to become angry, for anger does not bring about the righteous life that God desires. Therefore, get rid of all moral filth and the evil that is so prevalent, and humbly accept the word planted in you, which can save you. Do not merely listen to the word, and so deceive yourselves. Do what it says. Those who listen to the word but do not do what it says are like people who look at their faces in a mirror and, after looking at themselves, go away and immediately forget what they look like.

James 1.19–24

connected with the gathering of the church on a Sunday to worship Jesus. James, for instance, knew that those outside the Church would watch Christians and try to decide whether the risen Jesus was real, was good, and was worth following. He was aware that they wouldn't be impressed at all by churchgoing, Scripture-reading and praying. But a genuinely impressive sight would be a Monday-to-Saturday lifestyle which showed evidence that God had changed them.

Then, as now, it was useless to arrive at church on a Sunday, sing the right religious words, share bread and wine, then go away and behave as if it made no difference whatever to life at work, at home or at leisure. There must be integrity in a Christian life if it is going to be worth following Jesus at all. Just as the things we wear give away the fact that we belong to the twenty-first century, so our everyday life should display signs that we belong to Jesus. The way we talk, react to situations and form relationships should make people think, 'I'll bet that person is a Christian. I must find out more.'

James gave three practical signs by which Christians could be marked out as different, and they are as fresh today as they were then. The first is that 'everyone should

> As water reflects your face, so your heart reflects you.
>
> *Proverbs 27.19*

be quick to listen and slow to speak'. People sum us up by what comes out of our mouths, whether it is gossip, or language that doesn't fit comfortably alongside the language we use when we speak to God, or simply saying too much, too loud, for too long. We don't want people to say, 'I can't believe she or he goes to church after what I've just heard.'

When we are in conversation, we tend to listen to the first half of what someone says, and guess the rest, because we are trying to work out how we are going to reply. Would it be possible to develop a reputation as the one who is prepared to hear people out and find the best solution, rather than being the loudest or the most persistent? What would happen on the street where you live if you became the one with the reputation for not just saying hello, but remembering your neighbours' names and being interested in what they are doing?

The second sign is to 'be slow to become angry'. We have to deal with our anger somehow, because every single human being becomes angry – if not with someone else, then turned in on himself or herself. How we deal with that anger – whether it

> We are mirrors of God, created to reflect him. Even when the water is not calm, it reflects the sky.
>
> *Ernesto Cardenal, priest and poet, born 1925*

explodes in a violent way, or gets talked out in a controlled way – displays whether the peace of God for which we all pray is in control of our lives in theory or in practice.

And the third is to do with 'being rid of moral filth and evil'. This is going to express itself in the kind of jokes that people associate with us. It will be seen in the way we talk about people of other races or the opposite sexual

> Lord you are my lover, my longing, my flowing stream, my sun, and I am your reflection.
>
> *Mechtilde of Magdeburg, nun, 1220–80*

orientation. It will have an impact on which television programmes we watch, the computer games we play, and the magazines we read.

The Bible writers urge us to be at large in the world – shopping in its stores, dancing in its clubs, travelling on its roads, eating at its tables, and flirting behind its bike-sheds. But they expect us to be doing so in a way that is consistent with our friendship with Jesus, not one that leaves the stains of all we know is wrong in our world smeared over us. Look in the mirror! See yourself the way you are seen!

Detox: Take a look at your behaviour over the past few weeks as if you were looking in a mirror. See yourself the way others have seen you, particularly thinking about what you have said when silence would have been a better option, the way you have dealt with your anger, and the way you have spent your leisure time. If there are things that you need to apologize to God for, detox them now.

Lord God, teach me when to speak and when to be silent; when to watch and when to turn away; when to try to change a situation and when to leave quietly. And so may I never be ashamed to admit that I am a Christian. Amen.

Day 11

Enjoy goodness

The New Testament is full of images of light and darkness. And they weren't new ideas even then – for their first hearers they already had traditional associations. Light was a symbol of joy, blessing and life. Darkness stood for sorrow, death and evil. However, the Bible brought something different to these images. The ancient pagan writers showed light and darkness locked in a battle which either side might win. But the New Testament makes it clear that because of what Jesus has done – living, dying, rising again – light is already triumphant.

At the start of John's Gospel he writes, 'The light shines on in the dark, and the darkness has never mastered it.' Mastered has two meanings: not only is it impossible for the dark to conquer the light, it hasn't even been able to understand it. John goes on, 'Light has come into the world, but people loved darkness instead of light because their deeds were evil. Anyone who does evil hates the light, and will not come into the light for fear that his deeds will be shown up.' One of the purposes of Jesus' ministry was that the distinction between light and darkness should be absolutely clear.

It is human nature to find darkness more alluring than light. I've known that for years! As a boy, an apple stolen from the neighbour's garden tasted fantastic. The one my mother put in my packed lunch – I

> The light shines on in the dark, and the darkness has never mastered it.
>
> *John 1.5*

could take it or leave it! As a teenager, the sex that the vicar told me was forbidden seemed irresistibly alluring. The rich friendships that were available all around me – I took them for granted! As an adult, I go to the newsagent and walk very slowly past the tabloid newspapers because I'm keen to see which celebrity has been caught with drugs up his nose, or bribes down his pocket, and someone else's wife in his bed. The respectable newspaper that I actually buy – well, I've got to have some excuse to go into the shop!

Here is my servant, whom I uphold,
my chosen one in whom I delight;
I will put my Spirit on him
and he will bring justice to the nations.
He will not shout or cry out,
or raise his voice in the streets.
A bruised reed he will not break,
and a smouldering wick he will not snuff out.
In faithfulness he will bring forth justice . . .
I, the Lord, have called you in righteousness;
I will take hold of your hand.
I will keep you and will make you
to be a covenant for the people
and a light for the Gentiles.

Isaiah 42.1–3, 6

So here is the question behind today's detox: If darkness is so very appealing, why follow the light? To struggle with that we need to find out what Jesus meant when he said he was 'the light of the world'. He was quoting from Isaiah, who was looking forward to a great leader, the hope of the Jewish people: 'Here is my servant, whom I uphold, my chosen one in whom I delight; I will . . . make you to be a covenant for the people and a light for the Gentiles.'

Isaiah tells us three thrilling things about the Servant, the light of the world, which make him so compelling that darkness loses its lure. First, he says: 'A bruised reed he will not break, and a smouldering wick he will not snuff out.' Among the people of darkness, when you mess up you're lost. If you're weak, you're at the back of the queue. If you fail, you're on your own. But the light of the world is different. If you see yourself as a candle which is spluttering and failing, the light of the world will tend the wick, reshape the wax, cajole the flame back into life, and persist with what is valuable in you until it comes alive again. You don't get that kind of care among the people of the darkness. They would snuff you out and start with a new candle. Choose the light of life!

The second thing Isaiah says of the Servant is that he will faithfully bring forth justice. He will not falter until justice is established. Among the people of darkness, humans become worth what they are worth in the marketplace. If you live in a poor country, you're worth what you can be exploited for. If you're rich, you become obsessed by the shop bargain and blind to the appalling conditions some worker in the southern hemisphere endures in order for you to get things cheap. But the Servant is one in whom the poor can put their hope, because he works for justice. And he is one in whom the rich can trust, for he can release them from the burden of always wanting more. You don't get that kind of determination to do what is right among the people of the darkness. Choose the light of life!

> Goodness is stronger than evil;
> love is stronger than hate;
> light is stronger than darkness;
> life is stronger than death;
> victory is ours through him
> who loved us.
>
> Desmond Tutu, Archbishop of Cape Town, born 1931

And lastly, Isaiah puts wonderful promises in the mouth of God: 'I, the Lord, have called you in righteousness. I will take hold of your hand.' In Jesus, God is not merely a light on the horizon towards whom I stumble optimistically. Nor a ferocious light so dazzling that it would burn me up if I tried to approach. Nor a headlight which illuminates the way ahead and leaves me to do what I think is best. Rather, God is one who is walking alongside me every step of the way. In one hand he holds a lamp giving precisely as much light as I need to make the next move, and in the other hand he holds my hand. Choose the light of life!

Is the darkness appealing? Yes, of course it is. But darkness is where you go to develop your negatives. Jesus offered himself as the light of the world. As the one who coaxes the vulnerable back into life. As the one who will not finish his work until justice is done for all people. As the one who is there to hold our hands through whatever difficulty lies ahead. In him it is possible to rediscover the goodness of goodness!

> To try too hard to make people good is one way to make them worse; the only way to make them good is to be good.
>
> *George MacDonald, novelist, 1824–1905*

Which do you choose? For me there's no contest.

Detox: Go out into the world and do good! Be outrageously good! Make people's heads turn with the unexpectedness of it. Make goodness seem irresistible, and watch to see whether people catch the habit and pass it on. Add value to people's lives with the sheer fun of increasing the amount of virtue in the world. Do it secretly, so that no one knows where it is coming from, and chuckle at their surprise. Make this a way of scattering the darkness and, in the company of Jesus, unreservedly enjoying the light.

Light of the world, take my hand and lead me through life so that, in your company, I may be reminded of the goodness of goodness.

Day 12

Be generous

Hundreds of years ago, the kings of Wessex, Mercia and the other small kingdoms that now make up the United Kingdom were coming to a Christian faith one by one. In those days, when a king became a Christian his closest followers did the same whether they liked it or not! So when the king ordered his knights to be baptized they often held their right hands out of the water as they were immersed in it. The logic of this was that every part of them was baptized except the hand in which they held their sword. So if a crisis ever arose they felt free to kill an enemy without feeling constrained by the morals of their Christian faith.

Set aside a tenth of all that your fields produce each year . . . Exchange your tithe for silver, and take the silver with you and go to the place the Lord your God will choose. Use the silver to buy whatever you like: cattle, sheep, wine or other fermented drink, or anything you wish. Then you and your household shall eat there in the presence of the Lord your God and rejoice . . . At the end of every three years, bring all the tithes of that year's produce and store it in your towns, so that the Levites (who have no allotment or inheritance of their own) and the aliens, the fatherless and the widows who live in your towns may come and eat and be satisfied, and so that the Lord your God may bless you in all the work of your hands.

Deuteronomy 14.22–29

I sometimes think how convenient it would be if we were given the option of being 95 per cent Christian, leaving us the freedom to act in a completely self-centred way with one small section of our lives. For example, I am sure that some of us would much prefer to hold our wallets and purses out of the waters of baptism.

We tend to work out how much it costs to live, then budget for our families, our future needs and some treats. It is after doing those sums that we decide what we can spare for God's work from what is left. No wonder we have to grit our teeth in order to be generous.

It is a complete contrast to the way God's people arranged their finances in the Old Testament. For them giving time was party time! And, writing in the New Testament, Paul told those who were making financial sacrifices so the Lord's work could grow that 'God loves a cheerful giver'. (The word literally means 'a hilarious giver' which gives a picture of people roaring with laughter at their own generosity.)

The reason they could enjoy giving is that they had planned in advance what they would give to God. Having set it aside to be God's own, they no longer had to steel themselves, but could relish improving the lives of those around them. It was a simple and practical thank you to God.

The same signs are in evidence today. Shrivelled-up, resentful Christians are shrivelled-up, resentful givers. Open-hearted, worshipful Christians are open-hearted, worshipful givers. Christians who delight in knowing God's love also delight in the blessing of giving something back to the one who has given them everything.

Frankly, I do not know whether one tenth of what we earn, which is what the Hebrews of the Old Testament offered, is still the right figure for today. It does have the advantage that it costs just as much to give a tenth whether

> Each of you should give what you have decided in your heart to give, not reluctantly or under compulsion, for God loves a cheerful giver.
>
> *2 Corinthians 9.7*

a person is extremely wealthy or just scraping by. When you consider the goodness of God, who emptied his home of its greatest treasure on our behalf, I suppose the only proper answer to the question of how much we should give is: more than we can afford.

What happened to the tenth that the Hebrew people gave? First, it was spent on worship that was thrilling, involving friends and families, children and adults, food and music.

So seek out occasions when generosity can involve pleasure. If your giving involves money being transferred from one bank account to another without any noticeable sign that it has happened, invent your own occasional celebration to remind you of the goodness of God.

> May your bounty teach me greatness of heart. May your magnificence stop me being mean. Seeing you a prodigal and open-handed giver, let me give unstintingly like a king's son, like God's own.
>
> *Helder Camara, Archbishop of Recife, Brazil, 1909–99*

However, the eating and drinking involved when the Hebrews gave their 'tithe' did not happen in a greedy way. It was shared. The Levites, one of the groups that benefited from their gifts, were worship leaders. They relied totally on the generosity of God's people, just as churches today need money to be given so that they can be effective. The other beneficiaries were refugees, orphans and widows. Before the days when governments provided for people who could not fend for themselves, these were men, women and children who either relied on the generosity of God's people or starved. And still today giving money so that the poor can emerge from poverty is a crucial part of giving to God.

Does charity begin at home? Absolutely not for those who have taken their place in the Kingdom of God! God did not decide that charity begins at home and invest his love in the heavenly host. If he had done so, an entire needy world would have come to ruin. The astonishing generosity of God is shown in the fact that he decided to invest his greatest treasure in a foreign place – our planet.

I have been thinking about this a lot this month because I have had an unexpected windfall from my savings account. I have decided to give a proportion of it away first and then decide what to do with the rest. That means I have got a lovely little sum to do good with. I don't know which cause it is going to go to yet, but deciding is going to be very enjoyable. That money is going to improve someone's life dramatically and they don't even know it. What fun! It could be hilarious!

> You can give without loving, but you cannot love without giving.
>
> *Amy Carmichael, missionary to Asia, 1867–1951*

If you really believe that everything you have comes from the Lord, start by deciding what will go back thankfully to him, and let everything else drop into place behind it. Gather up everything you own, wallet and all, and baptize it in dedication to God.

Detox: Fetch your wallet or purse and completely empty it onto a table – money, photographs, cards, information, everything! What do the contents reveal about your priorities, relationships, values and generosity? What will you need to change in the way you organize your money if giving is to become a joy?

Lord God, you have given me your greatest treasure. What would it please you to receive from me? Amen.

Day 13

Face up to embarrassment

You are in Jerusalem, it's AD 31, and the atmosphere is heady. The Christian Church is going through a time of rapid growth, and every day brings a new excitement. The greatest joy is sharing your life with those who have the same faith. You fund what you do as a church by selling your possessions and living communally. You are constantly meeting, eating and talking about Jesus. Answers to prayer leave you awestruck. Everyone likes you, and the highlight of each day is to meet in the temple to praise God.

The temple is the ideal setting – big and beautiful enough to lift your spirits to God, especially the dazzling gateway.

One day Peter and John were going up to the temple at the time of prayer – at three in the afternoon. Now a man crippled from birth was being carried to the temple gate called Beautiful, where he was put every day to beg from those going into the temple courts. When he saw Peter and John about to enter, he asked them for money. Peter looked straight at him, as did John. Then Peter said, 'Look at us!' So the man gave them his attention, expecting to get something from them. Then Peter said, 'Silver or gold I do not have, but what I have I give you. In the name of Jesus Christ of Nazareth, walk.' Taking him by the right hand, he helped him up, and instantly the man's feet and ankles became strong. He jumped to his feet and began to walk.

Acts 3.1–8

It would be perfect, were it not for an embarrassment that you face every time you enter. Beside the temple's Beautiful Gate is an awkward, messy distraction. A beggar sits there day after day, asking you for money every time you pass. He has been crippled since birth, and the begging bowl in front of him is his only means of subsistence. You don't want to see ugliness because you are on your way to worship, and you prefer to fill your mind with lofty-wafty, oddly-godly thoughts.

But this wretched embarrassment won't go away. You try to pray him away; he's still there. You discuss the problem; he doesn't budge. You have a quiet word with the temple authorities; no good!

What you fail to realize is that God is saying to you, 'How many times do I have to put this poor scrap of a man in front of you until you recall what Jesus said: "I am anointed to preach good news to the poor, to proclaim freedom for the prisoners, recovery of sight for the blind, release for the oppressed."?' There is nothing about those words which is either lofty-wafty or oddly-godly! Do something!'

> Religion that God our Father accepts as pure and faultless is this: to look after orphans and widows in their distress and to keep oneself from being polluted by the world.
>
> James 1.27

You put this out of your mind as often as you can, until one day the man asks for money one time too many, and it breaks you. You wheel round in fury and yell, 'Look at us!' Or perhaps it's not like that. Perhaps you turn slowly because your heart has melted and with great sympathy you say, 'Look at us!' Or maybe you feel guilty that you have no loose change because all your cash is in a purse that the church shares, and with an exasperated apology you pull out your empty pockets and say, 'Look at us!' Whatever the reason, this is the day that the penny drops.

Or rather, the day when the penny didn't drop! Money was exactly what Peter and John didn't have. They discovered that they had four practical things instead. They had a compulsion to do something that had come from the name of Jesus. They had a right hand to hold out in touch, compassion and help. They had a determination that, although they couldn't solve all the man's problems, they could give him the means to become strong within himself and face the next phase. And they had a decision not to disguise their embarrassment any more – this time they were going to act.

And now I need to tell you about something that troubles me. I live close enough to my church to make it a pleasant walk every Sunday from my home to the lofty-wafty. But I force myself to keep my eyes on the pavement and my mind on the service as I make my way to the oddly-godly. I do this because my church has embarrassments on its doorstep, just as the temple did. There are homes for the elderly where I know without a doubt that some residents never have visitors. And there is accommodation where people who have fled their homes and are seeking asylum in Britain are housed

I was hungry, and you formed a humanities group to discuss my hunger. I was imprisoned, and you crept off quietly to your chapel and prayed for my release. I was naked, and in your mind you debated the morality of my appearance. I was sick, and you knelt and thanked God for your health. I was homeless, and you preached to me of the spiritual shelter of the love of God. I was lonely, and you left me alone to pray for me. You seem so holy, so close to God. But I am still very hungry, and lonely, and cold.

John Stott, Christian leader, born 1921

with very poor hospitality. And there are people walking the streets who are evidently in a state of confusion, or looking for shelter and company.

Silver or gold I do not have (although for different reasons from Peter and John). But neither do I have their miraculous powers. So what have I got to offer, in company with the rest of my congregation, that might make it worth saying, 'Look at us!'?

> Your theology is what you are when the talking stops and the action starts.
>
> Colin Morris, broadcaster, born 1928

We might be able to answer that question if we take seriously the four things that Peter and John had. Do we feel compelled to act because of the name of Jesus Christ? (We certainly call ourselves by the name 'Christian', so this is how we discover whether it has any real meaning.) Are we holding out a right hand in touch, compassion and help? (We need to question the sincerity of our worship if it does not happen in the context of a practical response to local needs.) Are we giving people a platform on which to stand so that they can find the strength to tackle their problems? (That is rather different from simply giving handouts of meals and secondhand clothes.) Have we got the will to admit our embarrassment and do something?

Those questions have been the most challenging part of my 40 day detox. And you?

Detox: What embarrassments come between you and your lofty-wafty worship? Are there ways of addressing them that are more imaginative than spending silver and gold?

Lord God, my right hand is yours. Before I next lift it to pray, may I hold it out to help. Amen.

Day 14

Seek purity

I have a nightmare that I will get to heaven and discover that every human has a clock which registers the way they have spent their lives. The hands will twirl backwards an hour for every occasion on which we have had a thought that was not pure. Yours will probably tremble into movement every few days. Jesus will be using mine as a fan!

In Israel and Palestine, at each of the sites at which the major events of Jesus' life took place, a chapel has been built. Beautifully designed and sensitive to their environment, they use colour, shape and symbol in a way that helps pilgrims reflect on the life of Jesus. One of them is at the summit of the hill that has traditionally been associated with the Sermon on the Mount. It is an octagonal building, full of light, with large windows in each wall giving spectacular views over Galilee. Above each of the eight windows is carved one of the beatitudes – the sayings of Jesus that congratulate those who have discovered the way of true happiness.

As I walked into the chapel some years ago the sun was cascading in and a vivid shaft fell directly on the words, 'Blessed are the pure in heart, for they will see God.' It made them seem to leap straight from the wall and into my conscience. I stood paralysed for a moment, profoundly ashamed about the jokes that make me laugh, the thoughts that distract me, and the difference

> Blessed are the pure in heart, for they will see God.
>
> *Matthew 5.8*

between the life that people see me live and the life going on in my head.

Why did Jesus say that it was pure people who would see God? Why not prayerful people or forgiven people? Because to be pure in heart (or pure in personality, as his first audience would have understood it) is dependent on how we look at people, how we interpret things, and what labels we give to those who cross our path.

If you look at someone and all you see is skin of a different colour, then you are not looking with a pure eye. A pure eye looks deep into a person and appreciates him or her for the goodness within them. An impure eye looks at the surface and makes instant judgements based on suspicion, fear and the age-old traditions that drive people apart. And when that happens, the impure heart has lost the chance to glimpse God in that person. It is rarely on the surface that the image of God is to be found in a human; it is usually deep within and takes time to be appreciated. But it is there. It is always there!

> 'I will be a Father to you, and you will be my sons and daughters,' says the Lord Almighty. Since we have these promises, dear friends, let us purify ourselves from everything that contaminates body and spirit, perfecting holiness out of reverence for God.
>
> 2 Corinthians 6.18—7.1

A pornographic picture shows you someone's flesh in a way that is designed to titillate or encourage lust. How can that come from the camera of someone pure in heart? Of course, this does not mean that all pictures of the human flesh that God created are pornographic. The artist and the viewer who are pure in heart have eyes that go beyond flesh and see the beauty and dignity with which God has blessed humanity. They show and see a soul laid bare and, through that, understand more of the essence of being human. In that we certainly glimpse the image of God. And what a blessing! But there is nothing pure about a picture in which all we see is the cheapness of humans as objects, and the abuse of young people because they are portrayed as sexually available. We will never see God in pornography because we are never given the chance.

If you laugh at or joke about someone who has a stammer, all you can recognize in that person is a label that reads 'disability'. That kind of impure laugh denies you the blessing of seeing God in a person, waiting to be revealed below the surface. And the same is true about laughter that insults someone who is elderly, or homosexual, or Asian, or any of a thousand other targets.

> Not to be jealous, not to be puffed up, not to act heedlessly, not to seek what does not belong to one, not to rejoice over some injustice, not to plan evil – what is this and its like if not the continuous offering to God of a heart that is perfect and truly pure, a heart kept free of all disturbance?
>
> *John Cassian, monk, 360–435*

Practise being pure in heart! Make a habit of looking at the people you meet in a new way. Look beyond the surface and ask, 'Where is God dwelling in this person?' Faced with an annoying shop assistant who is unnecessarily unhelpful, choose not to snap back with a cynical reply. Instead ask, 'Where is the image of God? Why does God love him or her? What damage or sadness in their life has made them act like this? Can I make a difference?' When you begin to see workers with that kind of purity, you begin to see God.

Faced with a traffic jam that threatens to snarl up your entire day's programme, choose not to lose your temper and swear secretly in your soundproof car. Instead ask, 'Where is God in all this? What is he trying to teach me? What could he do to change the lives of all the people fuming in the cars around me? And since God loves them so much, could I pray for them?' When you see drivers with that kind of purity, you begin to see God.

Try it! It may not be possible, because it is extremely difficult. Certainly Jesus would not have said, 'Congratulations!' to those who can do it, if it were an easy thing to do. But for people who can develop a pure heart the reward is tremendous, because all that previously seemed mere flesh and bone will become transformed into something that is ablaze with God's beauty. Ablaze!

> It is a pleasant thing to behold the light, but sore eyes are not able to look upon it. The pure in heart shall see God, but the defiled in conscience shall rather choose to be buried under rocks than to behold the presence of Jesus Christ.
>
> *Anne Bradstreet, poet, 1612–72*

Detox: As strangers flit through your life – on television, on advertising hoardings, or just passers by – try to look at them with a pure eye: 'Where is God in this and what is he saying?' Practise distinguishing between images and words that prompt you to rejoice in the goodness of God, and those on which it is better not to dwell.

Lord God, I am bombarded by pictures that are purely worldly. But I would like to be someone who sees the world purely. Reveal yourself to me, I pray. Amen.

Day 15

Choose wisely

I've got a new thermos flask. It keeps hot things hot and cold things cold. It's standing next to my computer, ready for my mid-morning break. In it, I've got two cups of coffee. And a choc ice.

Boom boom!

Some things don't mix! That is the simple and straightforward secret of leading a life that is holy. Keep the hot things hot and the cold things cold.

That is not to say that we should keep the religious part of our lives separate from the secular part. If we did, it would seem as if there were something odd about being a Christian, and nothing could be further from the truth. The moments of our lives when we are focused explicitly on God are an essential part of the way he has designed humans to operate. They are given to us as a natural part of the way we survive from Monday to Saturday, not

> Prepare your minds for action; be self-controlled; set your hope fully on the grace to be given you when Jesus Christ is revealed. As obedient children, do not conform to the evil desires you had when you lived in ignorance. But just as he who called you is holy, so be holy in all you do; for it is written: 'Be holy, because I am holy.' Since you call on a Father who judges each person's work impartially live your lives as strangers here in reverent fear.
>
> 1 Peter 1.13–17

just quirks peculiar to Sunday. So talk, eat, sleep, *pray*, work, laugh, kiss, *worship*, shop, drink, exercise, *praise*, have sex, breathe! There is nothing special or odd about religious activities. They are the context in which all the other activities make sense. They are what help make ordinary living into holy living.

Holy living is the way the Bible describes the difference between making all your choices in a Christian way, and making them as if God had no impact on your life. Being holy means being set apart. In the temple where God was worshipped centuries ago, there were some items of furniture and vessels that were not to be touched, not even to be approached. They were holy for God, set apart with absolute reverence to be his alone. So even then it was clear that some things don't mix. The perfection of God and the tawdry, selfish, corrupted thoughts of humans don't mix. They are coffee and choc ice. Set yourself apart from thoughts and actions like that, the New Testament tells us. Be holy!

> Do not conform any longer to the pattern of this world, but be transformed by the renewing of your mind. Then you will be able to test and approve what God's will is – his good, pleasing and perfect will.
>
> Romans 12.2

This is one of the most complicated challenges of our detox. God wants us to do two things at the same time. He wants us to be part of our society, engaging with and enjoying everything and everybody the world has to offer. But, at the same time, he wants us to be set apart, to be recognizably different from people who are not Christians. In one of his letters in the New Testament, Peter writes, 'Do not conform to the evil desires you had when you lived in ignorance.' How do you do the two things at one time? How do you keep hot things hot and cold things cold?

Fortunately, Peter went on to answer the question. First, 'Prepare your minds for action; be self-controlled.' Be part of your society in every way! Read the same newspapers as those who do not hold following God as a priority; watch the same TV programmes; enjoy the same nightclubs; do the same jobs. But go into each one with your mind prepared. Read the paper having decided, 'I won't be told what to think, but I'll take what I see here to God and find out what he thinks.' That's simple holiness. Go to your favourite club thinking to yourself, 'I'm going to have a great time here in a self-controlled way. I won't be pressurized into doing anything. God and I will be making decisions together tonight.' That's holiness too.

Peter's second answer is, 'Live your lives as strangers here in reverent fear.' As a Christian, your true home is in heaven. In heaven it will be effortless and easy to make good choices. While some swagger about the earth, making choices as if the planet is theirs to treat as they wish for 70 years, Christians should spend their time here in a different way. Treat the earth like a responsible visitor. Don't act as if you are on a lads' holiday in the Mediterranean, strutting around aggressively with a pint of lager slopping out of the glass, down your beetroot red arms and onto your patriotic boxer shorts. Instead act like an ambassador for your homeland in heaven, with the courtesy of someone who is in a strange land. Behave in a way that will make those you meet

> Every day the choice between good and evil is presented to us in simple ways.
>
> *W. E. Sangster, preacher, 1900–60*

> Wisdom lies in learning not to shrink from anything that may be in store for us, but so to grasp the master key of life as to be able to turn everything to good and fruitful account.
>
> *Caroline Stephen, writer, 1834–1909*

think well of your heavenly home, enjoy your company, and feel that their land has been enriched by your visit. It wasn't money that bought your holiday ticket; it was the death of Jesus himself. So don't take your presence here lightly. Do good with it.

Be enthusiastically and committedly part of this world, and live for every joy there is to be had in it. But keep the hot things hot and the cold things cold. Live in the world in a way which is holy, with your mind prepared, like an ambassador for God.

Detox: Make a list of all the places to which you will go during the next few days – homes, workplaces, entertainment centres, places of worship. Prepare your mind! In each case, think about what it will mean to be fully engaged with the people and activities there, but in such a way that you are a worthy ambassador for God. If you have made bad choices in these circumstances before, make a conscious decision that this time will be different.

God of my life, teach me to make good choices – red hot in the face of opportunity; ice cool in the face of temptation. Amen.

Detox your past

Day 16

Confess

I was staying with a friend in a beautiful valley in Somerset. When I went to the bathroom I discovered that the lid of my shampoo had come loose and emptied the contents into my travel bag. Grumpily I washed everything and was left with a bag full of soap. I decided that the best thing to do was to step into the shower with it and rinse the whole lot out. Doing so, I accidentally spilled some shampoo on the cream-coloured carpet. It didn't exactly stain it, but the carpet was definitely discoloured and I couldn't remove the mark. I looked at it again and again, thinking, 'Can I get away with this, or should I confess what I've done?' Eventually I decided that, as it was in a shadowy corner of the bathroom, I could hide what I had done. All through breakfast I avoided the subject, but I felt distinctly uneasy.

However, there was something I had not taken into account – the extremely soft water in the rolling hills. In combination with a warm shower and a bottle full of shampoo it had reacted dramatically in the pipes. When we opened the front door, a vast cloud of soap suds had bubbled up out of the drain. It smothered the driveway, the lawn and the flower beds in froth. My friend gasped, 'Whatever has happened?' Of course, I

> If we claim to be without sin, we deceive ourselves and the truth is not in us. If we confess our sins, he is faithful and just and will forgive us our sins and purify us from all unrighteousness.
>
> 1 John 1.8–9

knew instantly. I had no choice but to confess what I had done wrong. All through the day I kept being reminded of those old men who used to walk through town centres with placards saying, 'Be sure your sins will find you out!'

> When I kept silent, my bones wasted away
> through my groaning all day long.
> For day and night your hand was heavy upon me;
> my strength was sapped as in the heat of summer.
> Then I acknowledged my sin to you
> and did not cover up my iniquity.
> I said, 'I will confess my transgressions to the Lord,'
> and you forgave the guilt of my sin.
> Therefore let everyone who is godly
> pray to you while you may be found.
>
> *Psalm 32.3–6*

Of all the invisible toxins that stop us enjoying our lives to the full, the memory of things we have done wrong in the past is one of the most debilitating. But feelings of guilt are God's gift to us. They are his way of prompting us to do something to repair the damage. Curiously, the fact that we feel guilt does not show what terrible people we are; it reveals that we are morally responsible people who want to do better. One of the great joys of being a Christian is that Jesus has revealed the way to be completely free from the contamination. He says, 'I'll deal with that for you!'

When we bring to mind what we have done wrong and admit to God that we should not have done it, will it have an impact on the way God treats us? Absolutely not! God is infinitely merciful and gracious, and his love does not depend on what we do. However, naming something we have done as sinful can have a profound impact on the way we treat ourselves! It can turn us from people who are dragging burdens behind us into people who are travelling freely, loving God deeply and relating to people without unhappy memories of what has gone before.

Sometimes it is enough to confess to God what has happened and move on – for example, if you lose your temper with an infuriating stranger on a crowded train. We can trust God to heal the damage done to someone we will never see again. But losing your temper with someone with whom you have a continuing relationship requires a conversation with the person as well, because he or she needs to move on from the incident as much as you do. A failure to confess will reappear in another form later in life, as surely as soap suds gurgle up from a drain!

> To confess our sins is to accuse ourselves of them; quite a different thing from merely telling them.
> Maud Petre, writer, 1863–1942

Charles Wesley wrote in his hymn 'O for a thousand tongues' that 'He breaks the power of cancelled sin'. Some people find themselves talking to God about the same sin over and over again without ever letting go of it, as if even confessed sin still has power over them. This can hold us back because behind it lies uncertainty about God's mercy. It may be that in these circumstances saying, 'I should not have done it', to someone else can be a means of moving on from sins long past. The ancient tradition of confessing remorse to a priest or a Christian friend, and hearing them say, 'God forgives', may prove helpful. But even more helpful is the discovery that the psalm-writer made – that the forgiveness of God is something that can make our whole selves better. Body, soul and relationships – all of them can be relieved when God responds to this detox.

Actions have consequences. Even forgiven actions have consequences. Confessing what we have done wrong to

God will leave us at peace with him forever. But we need to be realistic about the fact that it will not turn back the clock and make the impact of the sin disappear from the lives of those who were involved. Confessing to God the stupidity of a flirtation that broke up a relationship will mean that you are forgiven, but it will not mean that the relationship can be expected to resume as if nothing had happened. It may take years of care, truth and trust to allow those involved to be at peace with each other. And the relationship may never return to its previous joyfulness, because people forgive at different speeds and with a different intensity. But there are some things that remain true through it all: faithfulness is better than disloyalty, truth is better than lying, forgiveness is better than animosity. And God will remain faithful, true and forgiving until the end that has no ending.

> He breaks the power of cancelled sin,
> he sets the prisoner free;
> his blood can make the foulest clean;
> his blood availed for me.
>
> *Charles Wesley, hymn writer, 1707–88*

Detox: Write down things that you, in your recent or distant past, have done wrong and now regret. Divide them into three groups. If they have no power left to damage you or anyone else, cross them off. If they still disturb you, confess them to the all-forgiving God. If they still damage your relationship with someone else, consider what conversation you might need to have in order to move on.

Lord Jesus, you are more ready to forgive than I am to confess. Heal, I pray, the damage that I have done – to those I love, to those I will never see again, and to you. Amen.

Day 17

Let go of failures

I've just moved into a new home. I've not gone far – less than a mile. But moving house is always unsettling. I get in the car and drive to the supermarket. Then I drive back, turn off the engine, get out of the car, and realize that I have gone to my old house instead of my new one. Not just once; I do it again and again! What is wrong with me? It's as if I have a homing instinct that takes me back to a place I don't want to go to.

To be honest, my whole life is like that. I wish I could do something about it. There are certain things that I know are not good for me. They are things that make God's world function poorly: extravagance, laziness, selfishness. I tell myself that I've moved on from them, but then I get distracted by something and I go back without even noticing what has happened.

I seem to go through the same processes again and again. Letting God down, realizing it, repenting, starting over, having good intentions, letting God down, realizing it, repenting . . . and so on. I feel as though I need someone constantly praying to God on my behalf. Someone

> I have the desire to do what is good, but I cannot carry it out. For what I do is not the good I want to do; no, the evil I do not want to do – this I keep on doing . . . What a wretched man I am! Who will rescue me from this body of death? Thanks be to God – through Jesus Christ our Lord!
>
> *Romans 7.18, 19, 24–25*

who has managed to break that cycle of continually going back to things we want to put behind us. If I can't have that, I will be praying for forgiveness for the same things my whole life long without ever being sure it is having any impact. Every hymn I sing will be spoilt by not being sure that God is listening to me, because he might be still angry at what I have done.

And into this need (which seems to be shared by the whole of humankind) wonderfully, magnificently, comes Jesus. When I feel I need someone who is on my side, telling God constantly about my needs, and explaining to him that really I am loveable after all, who is there for me? He is!

It's not what you know, it's who you know! And when you know Jesus you really do have friends in high places.

> [Jesus] is able to save completely those who come to God through him, because he always lives to intercede for them. Such a high priest meets our need – one who is holy, blameless, pure, set apart from sinners, exalted above the heavens. Unlike the other high priests, he does not need to offer sacrifices day after day, first for his own sins, and then for the sins of the people. He sacrificed for their sins once for all when he offered himself . . . the Son who has been made perfect for ever.
>
> Hebrews 7.25–28

'He is able to save completely those who come to God through him, because he always lives to intercede for them,' the letter to the Hebrews tells us. He is on your side! That is a fact which transforms lives. He is on your side!

Why is it that Jesus can help us break the cycle of good intentions and bad habits when no one else can? Because he is a priest.

Oh! How disappointing!

The trouble is, we have been let down by priests time and time again. It's not their fault; they are just humans with all their weaknesses. No priest is able to break this circle of wrong-doing for us, because priests are no better than us. They have their own problems to deal with. Even if you are an archbishop you are not able to forgive someone their sins, because before you even get out of bed in the morning you have to confess to God the sins you yourself have done. We need someone better than that.

That is precisely why the man who wrote the letter to the Hebrews was so excited. He was able to assure his readers that Jesus is a priest who is better in every conceivable way. He is perfect. He is 'holy, blameless, pure, set apart from sinners'. He has never needed to come before God and say sorry, so he is the only person who can talk to God about our repentance and our worth with complete integrity. The Jewish Christians who first read these words must have been ecstatic. They would never have to go to the temple again to offer sacrifices of animals to God, because Jesus the high priest had offered himself as a sacrifice. A perfect sacrifice. Once and for all!

And you and me? All those embarrassments about things we did wrong years ago that ambush us. Forget it! Because of Jesus they are forgiven – past, present and future.

All those memories that make us cringe as we ask, 'Why, oh why, did I do that?' Let them go! They are in Jesus' hands now, and there are none safer.

All those worries we have about whether we have said the right thing to God in the right way. Relax! Jesus is in God's presence right now talking about you and me to God in a way more perfect than anyone on earth could ever manage.

Past failures are potent. Even

> Do not trust in your own righteousness; do not grieve about a sin that is past and gone; and keep your tongue and your belly under control.
>
> *Antony of Egypt, hermit, 251–356*

when they are forgiven, they can still exert a power. But Jesus has done everything it takes to emasculate them. So failures now only have as much hold over you as you let them have. Like Jacob Marley in Dickens' ghost story *A Christmas Carol*, the chain of your past that you drag around with you is a chain of your own making.

When memories of long-forgiven sins come back to haunt you, tell them that they have no right to assault you. In real words if it helps! Aloud if that's what it takes! Send them to Jesus, who has the authority to deal with them, and move on.

> The spectre raised a cry, and shook its chain with a dismal and appalling noise, and wrung its shadowy hands. 'You are fettered,' said Scrooge, trembling. 'Tell me why?' 'I wear the chain I forged in life,' replied the ghost. 'I made it link by link, and yard by yard; I girded it on of my own free will, and of my own free will I wore it.' Scrooge trembled more and more.
>
> *Charles Dickens, novelist, 1812–70*

No going back. I am in a new home. Onwards!

Detox: If reading this chapter has forced you to remember things you would rather forget, write them on a postcard. Put it in an envelope, seal it, address it to Jesus, and throw it away. If ever the guilt of them nags you again, swot it away as if it were a fly, and let it know that you do not want it back in your mind.

Lord Jesus, you have saved me from the damage done to me by sin. Now save me from the damage I do to myself. Amen.

Day 18

Look back

So then! You are in a car and you're driving west on the M4 motorway to get to somewhere near Gloucester. It's last Monday, and for the sake of argument let's say the car is a Ford Fiesta. You've been driving for two hours so you no longer have a hundred per cent concentration. You're late for a meeting, and, in fact, you don't even want to go to this meeting, and you're wondering whether it was a wise decision to go to it anyway. And as this is entirely hypothetical, let's say the car is red. And rusty. And usually parked outside my house!

Now imagine that at the M5 motorway turn-off you remember that last time you were here you took the wrong turning. And you urgently try to remember which wrong turning you took – did you stay on the motorway when you should have left, or did you leave the motorway when you should have stayed? You are happily confident you're in the correct lane until the very last moment, when you decide that you should be going the other way. So, at profound risk to your life (and, indeed, the life of every other motorist on the road), you veer into the other lane. And it's at that precise moment, when it's *just* too late to change back, that you realize you've made the wrong choice. And your heart slugs down into the chassis, because you remember from last time that when you take a wrong turning here it's miles and miles until you can turn round again.

You know that feeling? Me too!

I could pass an A level in lousy last-minute choices! The

> [Moses declared,] 'I have set before you life and death, blessings and curses. Now choose life, so that you and your children may live and that you may love the Lord your God, listen to his voice, and hold fast to him. For the Lord is your life.'
>
> *Deuteronomy* 30.19–20

result is that I am constantly going over things in my mind thinking, 'Have I made the right decision?'

In London there is a one-way system that you have to go through if you're driving from my house to Kew Gardens. As you get to the end of a big detour, there is a sign that says 'The North', and it points left. Underneath it there is a sign that says 'The South'. And it's pointing left as well. You would think it is difficult to go wrong! But I panicked because I wanted to go to Kew Gardens, which is west. So I turned right. I was in Woolworths car park!

The Bible tells us that God has chosen us. He didn't make a mistake when he did so, and he hasn't changed his mind since.

> You have been my hope, O Sovereign Lord,
> my confidence since my youth.
> From birth I have relied on you;
> you brought me forth from my mother's womb.
> I will ever praise you.
>
> *Psalm* 71.5–6

We think to ourselves: 'How can that be, when we let God down and let ourselves down so very often?' And the reply comes from God: 'That is not even relevant – you are a human being and I've chosen you because I love loving human beings.'

So we think to ourselves: 'How can that be, when I have

to face hurts and hardships that make me doubt everything I have ever believed?' And the reply comes from God: 'Choose the way of Jesus, because with his inspiration you will find the strength to endure.'

But we think to ourselves: 'How can I be sure that I have made the right choice?' And the reply comes from God: 'Look back at the road we have taken together. What have you learnt on the journey?'

The reason we can be sure we made the right choice when we decided to go through this life accompanied by the Spirit of Jesus is not because it has taken our hardships away, but because we have been through the catastrophes and the conflicts again and again, and we're still here, and we're still God's.

We've flooded the bathroom, and the world didn't come to an end, and our faith didn't come to an end either. We've fallen in and out of love with all the wrong people in all the wrong ways, and we're still alive, and Jesus is still alive in us. We've lost our jobs and our car keys and our health and our tempers, and we're still bearing up, and it's still God who is bearing us up. We've been through, 'Why why me?', and we've been through, 'Never never again!', and we've been through, 'Please please no!', and God is still here and has not let us go.

> Gratitude looks to the past, and love to the present; fear, avarice, lust and ambition look to the future.
>
> C. S. Lewis, writer, 1898–1963

Our doubts and fears are not at an end.

But you come over time to know that you have made the right choice when you have been in despair, and found yourself helped. When you have been hurt and heartbroken, and then healed. When you have given up all hope, and found yourself scraping through. When you've made all the wrong decisions, sometimes through rotten luck and sometimes because you knew it was sin but you did it anyway, and God is still there for you with open arms. When you're on the M4, driving helplessly past your turning saying, 'Drat, drat, drat, drat!' and God is sitting in the passenger seat beside you saying, 'Drat, drat, drat!' in a sympathetic echo.

You are reading this book because, one way or another, at some point in your life you have chosen Jesus, and Jesus has chosen you. No matter what other bad choices have featured in your life, those were good ones. Look back at the route he has taken you so far, and the lessons you have learnt as you reached this moment will sustain you. They will sustain you whether you find yourself on the M4 or on the M5. They will sustain

> In the spiritual journey we travel through the night towards the day. We walk not in the bright sunshine of total certainty but through the darkness of ignorance, error, muddle and uncertainty. We make progress in the journey as we grow in faith.
> *Christopher Bryant, monk, 1905–86*

you in Kew Gardens and they will sustain you in Woolworths car park. They will sustain you on earth, and they won't pass away even when you arrive in heaven.

Detox: Consider the choices that you have made recently. There may have been large ones connected with where you live and how you study or earn. There will certainly have been small ones made in shops and places of entertainment. Which of them were good ones and which not so good? How will the good ones give you confidence in God's direction; how will the bad ones require trust in God's desire to heal and restore his people?

God of all my days, as I look back may I be aware of your shadow beside me at every turn. And as I look forward may I trust your light before me in every decision. Amen.

Day 19

Put regrets behind you

I wonder what happened to Andrew! The last time we meet him in the Bible he is part of the group of Christians meeting in Jerusalem after Jesus' ascension, praying with utter commitment. But his relationship with Jesus did not begin with such uncompromising devotion; it began with simple curiosity.

He had been part of John the Baptist's group and might have stayed a quietly religious fisherman had not John pointed out Jesus and whispered, 'That is the one!' So Andrew and his friend follow Jesus at a distance, out of sight, intrigued. Suddenly Jesus catches sight of them, wheels round and says, 'Yes, can I help you?'

Their embarrassment is evident – the kind of awkwardness you feel when you are sitting on a bus looking at people's faces, and you catch the eye of someone who is looking back at you. There is an uncomfortable pause, and the only words Andrew can manage to stammer are, 'Where are you staying?' How banal!

So Jesus replies, 'Come and see!' And before they know

> When [Andrew and Philip heard what John said], they followed Jesus. Turning round, Jesus saw them following and asked, 'What do you want?' They said, 'Rabbi' (which means Teacher), 'where are you staying?' 'Come,' he replied, 'and you will see.' So they went and saw where he was staying, and spent that day with him.
>
> John 1.37–39

what they are doing, they are following. They are going and seeing. And it turns out to be amazing!

But it is hardly any time at all before Jesus says to Andrew and the others, 'Right, I'm leaving this place and going to Galilee. Are you following me or are you staying?' And suddenly they are faced with their first real decision. They can no longer have both Jesus and the life they are used to. The choice is simple – the dreary safety of what the rest of the world is doing, or him. They follow!

Somebody unsettled me last week by asking whether I ever regret the decision I made 20 years ago to follow Jesus with the same intensifying commitment that his first disciples did. To be honest, it was a daft question, and I knew precisely what to answer: 'Of course I do!' Barely a month goes by without me spending an hour thinking, 'You stupid man! What have you done?' My journey following Jesus has led me to a life working on behalf of the world's poorest communities. My schoolfriend decided at the same time to go and work in the City. He has just bought a yacht; I can't afford to get a basic mortgage. You would have regrets too, wouldn't you?

But then you catch sight of Jesus, striding up the hill as you follow at an ever slower pace. And he turns and asks, 'Are you part of this adventure or not?'

And you wearily reply, 'Well, what's the view like from the top of the hill?'

And he says, 'Come and see!' And before you know what you're doing, you're following. You're going and seeing. And it turns out to be amazing!

> Then [Jesus] said to them all: 'Those who would come after me must deny themselves and take up their cross daily and follow me. For those who want to save their lives will lose them, but those who lose their lives for me will save them.'
>
> *Luke 9.23–24*

Two years after his first tentative meeting with Jesus, Andrew's curiosity had taken him to a place he could not possibly have expected to go. He had left his job, security and family. He had gambled everything on following Jesus. And Jesus kept on inviting him to give more and more, until finally his demand was uncompromising. 'Anyone who does not take up his cross and follow me,' Jesus insisted, 'cannot be my disciple.'

This must have sent a shudder through Andrew, because a person who took up a cross was a condemned man on his way to his execution. Jesus was asking, 'How far are you prepared to go? Far enough to die with me?' By then death was a real possibility.

The further we go with Jesus the further he asks us to go. There is a bittersweet moment in the story of his ministry when he had given a talk that was so long and complicated that most of the audience gave up and walked away. Bitterly disappointed, Jesus turned to the disciples and asked, with a great sigh, 'What about you? Would you prefer to leave? You're free to go if you want to.'

And, facing up to their regrets, Andrew and his brother Peter must have realized that they had cut themselves off from their past so completely that they no longer had a choice. With words that wrapped together

> When Christ calls a man he bids him come and die.
>
> *Dietrich Bonhoeffer, theologian, executed for his resistance to Nazism, 1905–45*

sadness, resignation and determination, Peter replied, 'Well, where else could we go? It always was you or nothing. We have found the one who has the words of eternal life. We have found the Holy One of God. We have left ourselves with no choice but to keep following.' And for the hundredth time, or maybe the thousandth, he took up his cross and followed.

What is it about Jesus that allows us to take such a reckless gamble, staking everything on following him, even to death itself?

This Jesus is no mere teacher with a bright set of political or moral ideas. This Jesus is the Holy One of God. It is his hand that designed and formed the entire created order of time and space. It is his hand that has control over the future of our world and the potential of our lives. And his hand holds the map. It is the map of a Kingdom that will usher in the end of poverty, the end of violence and the triumph of justice. It is a good map.

> All the past we leave behind.
> We take up the task eternal
> and the burden, and the lesson.
> Conquering, holding, daring, venturing,
> so we go the unknown ways —
> Pioneers, O pioneers!
>
> Walt Whitman, poet, 1819–92

Following Jesus will start with simply being intrigued about him. He will accept that. It will lead us on roads where we make decisions that change our direction. He will expect that. It will take us to the point where we stake all we have on him. He will respect that.

He may lead me on paths which are not safe; he may throw me among strangers; he may take me to places where I recognize nothing. But he holds the map, and therefore I will follow.

He may make me confused; make my spirit weary; fill me with apprehension at what the future holds. But he holds the map, and therefore I will follow.

He may lead me to question all the things I used to be sure of; he may give me every indication of his plan for me then lead me abruptly to a closed door; he may put me through events whose significance will be a mystery until the very day I reach heaven. But he holds the map, and therefore I will follow.

I have no idea what the view is like from the top of the next hill. Let's go and find out!

Detox: What might you have been had you not decided to follow Jesus? Do you answer that question with relief or regret? After acknowledging that there were other possibilities, let them go, and begin to get excited about the view from the next hill that you and Jesus will climb together.

Lord of the journey, loosen my grip on all that might have been, so that I may not be dragged back by regret. Tighten my grasp of all that you want to lead me into, so that I may walk with you in trust and lively hope. Amen.

Day 20

Recycle your experiences

I have no one to blame but myself! I have been given a pair of rollerblades and last week, in a lunatic attempt to impress my teenage friends, I decided to skate to a party. It was a slow, uphill journey, but my arrival provoked all the entertainment I had hoped for. However, while I was at the party there was a shower of rain. It turned the gentle inclines of South London into the Cresta Run. The result was that my return journey in the early hours of the morning was quicker. Much, much quicker! And instead of ending at my front door, it ended in a hedge several metres past. A neighbour, bewildered by the sight of a pair of ankles erupting from the privet, pulled me out. Scratched in a thousand places I sat in a hot bath for half an hour trying to persuade myself that there were lessons to be learnt!

No matter how often it happens, I find myself astonished that when I cut myself, something mystical starts to happen deep inside my body. Cuts heal up all by themselves. I don't tell them to do it; they just get on with it. Bruises as black as an eclipse find their way back to my flesh's normal

> Rend your heart and not your garments. Return to the Lord your God, for he is gracious and compassionate, slow to anger and abounding in love . . . 'I will repay you for the years the locusts have eaten . . . You will have plenty to eat, until you are full, and you will praise the name of the Lord your God.'
>
> *Joel 2.13, 25–26*

colour. It seems that God has buried profoundly wonderful sources of healing deep in the natural order of things. I find that miraculous. It's as if God is so profoundly committed to healing that these things happen despite themselves.

God is a God whose heart is set on recycling. On a worldwide scale the carbon dioxide that we breathe out (it would kill us if we didn't get rid of it) is breathed in by the world's trees, which thrive on it and emit the oxygen that we need to survive. What a fantastic system of creation in balance!

A word that the Bible uses in connection with God is redemption. It means buying back, restoring the original value, bringing good out of bad. We know God is like that, because the planet he has put us on demonstrates it. The leaves that fall off the trees in autumn break down into their elemental goodness and enrich the earth to produce the beauty that thrusts into view in spring.

But it is not merely the natural world which God recycles. He recycles experiences as well. Nothing that happens in our lives need be wasted. There is always something that God wants us to learn. If we allow him to, he can recycle our mistakes, even the ones we regret deeply, to produce wisdom that enriches our lives. He can recycle our successes to generate advice for our friends. He can recycle sadness to produce sympathy for others. He can recycle good fortune to produce generosity. Experiences recycle on and on through our lives until, in the goodness of God, we are redeemed through death (the last and greatest healing) and come into his presence made perfect forever.

> The God of all grace, who called you to his eternal glory in Christ, after you have suffered a little while, will himself restore you and make you strong, firm and steadfast.
>
> 1 Peter 5.10

About 600 years before Jesus, an environmental catastrophe struck the Jews. A plague of locusts ripped through
their land, devastated their crops and brought them to the
brink of starvation. But in a context of complete desolation,
God told them through the prophet Joel, 'Don't be afraid
. . . I will repay you . . . You will have plenty to eat, until
you are full, and you will praise the name of the Lord.'

Everyone has disappointments, but they treat them in
one of two ways. For some people, failed ambitions, physical impediments or the inability to find a partner recycle
into something rich and generous. But others who
experience very similar things let them ferment into bitterness, cynicism or an inability to appreciate life. Discovering
the goodness of God in this recycling process does not happen automatically. We need to involve ourselves in the
process.

Joel explained that the vital difference involves allying
ourselves with God's desire to recycle, and playing our part
in the learning. Let's take an
example which might apply
to any one of us – a calamity
experienced while roller
blading! Either you get up
and say, 'Never again!' or
you throw your muddy
clothes in the washing
machine and think, 'How do
I adjust my braking tech-
nique so that doesn't happen
next time?'

Joel told the Jews that in
order to recycle their terrible
experience they needed to
return to God, not by saying
prayers and singing psalms,

> Be comforted then, for
> God leads into hell and out
> again; he makes us sad and
> joyful again; he gives death
> and also life, and after
> great storms he makes the
> sun shine again. Therefore
> wait patiently for the
> restoration of your bodies,
> and do not grow faint or
> weary in the race. See to it
> that the love in your hearts
> does not grow cold or die.
>
> *Jakob Hutter, Christian leader,*
> *1492–1536*

but by a complete change of lifestyle that would harmonize their lives with the natural order of things which God has established for his creation. They could sing as loud as they liked, but if the notes were not matched by a life actively encouraging love between people, it counted for nothing.

They could pray with all the fervour they could muster, but if they were not actively promoting a world of peace and justice, God was not impressed. They could rip their clothes apart with the sheer effort of calling out to God, but if it only changed their outsides, they could save themselves the repair bill.

We have a God who 'repays us for the years the locusts have eaten'. For those who seek meaning in all that befalls them, the restoration will far exceed the calamity. That is the power of recycling our experiences, a process that will finally lead us to heaven – the place from which we will look back and see the path which took us from birth, through learning, into healing.

> God (but only God) can transform evil into good, so that in retrospect (but only in retrospect) it is seen actually to have been good, without diminishing in the least the awful actuality of the evil it was at the time.
>
> *Frances Anderson, writer, born 1932*

Detox: Bring to mind some of the experiences of your past which seem a waste of time – people with whom you have now lost touch, projects that came to nothing, experiences that left you confused. Are you able to recycle what God has taught you into something that might be valuable to others?

O God, let me glimpse beyond the damage to the healing, and beyond the hurting to the learning, so that nothing that happens to me will be wasted. Amen.

Day 21

Be nostalgic

Here's another thing I can't stand! A fortune gets invested in improving a product, but when you try it you realize that you preferred the old, unimproved version. It's not just trivial matters; it can be really important things. Like gingernut biscuits! When I was young they were tough enough to break your teeth on them. The ginger was so overpowering that you had to drink a cup of tea to protect your mouth. Bliss! Recently those deadly words 'New Improved' appeared on the pack. I knew we were in trouble. Soft, bland, crumbly and nothing like a near-death experience!

While we're on the subject – records! Buying a record used to be an event. You came home from the shop with something substantial – black, beautifully covered and just the right weight. Where is the joy in bringing home a diddly CD that could fall down a drain or get left on the bus? When you're in the rain outside the shop door on the release date of *Sergeant Pepper's Lonely Hearts Club Band* do you want to go home with something in a little bag that people could mistake for a coaster? No! You want to swagger through the street with something as heavy as a dinner plate and as thick as a frisbee.

Those were the good old days! The scary thing is that, in 20 years' time, these will turn out to have been the good old days as well. It's a real challenge to Christians to know when we should embrace the future enthusiastically and when we should calm the pace of change. There is a place for both options. The church is going to look ridiculous if it doesn't address the new issues that the rest of the world is dealing with. But at the same time it is going to need the wisdom of people who remember what has happened in our history.

> When the builders laid the foundation of the temple . . . with praise and thanksgiving they sang to the Lord: 'He is good; his love to Israel endures for ever.' And all the people gave a great shout of praise to the Lord, because the foundation of the house of the Lord was laid. But many of the older . . . family heads, who had seen the former temple, wept aloud when they saw the foundation of this temple being laid, while many others shouted for joy. No one could distinguish the sound of the shouts of joy from the sound of weeping, because the people made so much noise.
>
> *Ezra 3.10–13*

Six centuries before Jesus, the Jews had suffered a terrible defeat in battle. They had been warned repeatedly that the alliances they were making would be their downfall, but they hadn't listened. They just assumed that being God's chosen people gave them rights to his protection that no one else had. So when Jerusalem was destroyed by the advancing armies of Babylon, and the temple that Solomon had built was flattened, they were bewildered, demoralized and dragged away into exile many miles from home. Men were castrated (including names that are familiar to us, such as Daniel). Women found themselves in prostitution (including names we know, such as Esther). It was a terrible era – biblical times were certainly not the good old days.

The worst blow for the Jews was that they believed they had lost their God. Their understanding at that time was that God lived in the temple at Jerusalem. So with the city destroyed and the temple wrecked, they believed that God had been left behind, homeless, and that they were finally on their own. It was a catastrophe.

> These things I remember as I pour out my soul:
> how I used to go with the multitude,
> leading the procession to the house of God,
> with shouts of joy and thanksgiving among the festive throng.
> Why are you downcast, O my soul?
> Why so disturbed within me?
> Put your hope in God, for I will yet praise him,
> my Saviour and my God.
>
> Psalm 42.4–6

But a remarkable piece of learning took place which has changed everything we know about God. The Jews began to realize that God was with them in Babylon just as he had been with them in Jerusalem. In fact, he was everywhere. This was a completely new concept. And because they felt his presence, they found that they were able to pray, to settle and to prosper. They didn't seek revolution; instead they started to work with the Babylonians. And when political changes took place, they engaged with their new rulers. Finally an emperor named Cyrus took control and pursued a policy of returning conquered peoples to their homelands. He did it because he thought that by doing so he would win God's approval. And so it was that after three generations the Jews found themselves on their way home.

They didn't all make the journey at once. And many of the younger generation didn't want to go since they felt that their home was where they lived, not the unknown land of which their grandparents spoke. But the first great home-coming was led by a man called Zerubbabel. (It's a mystery why his name is so little known when those who followed him, Ezra and Nehemiah, both had Bible books named after them. They must have had a better agent!) Their first priority was to build an altar so that they could start worshipping God straight away. After that, they began to build a temple around it. At the laying of the foundation stone they called out with thanksgiving to the Lord: 'He is good; his love endures forever.'

> We seem to know everything about the last twenty-four hours, but next to nothing about the last twenty-four years, let alone the last twenty-four centuries.
>
> Os Guinness, writer, born 1941

But then something interesting happened: 'Many of the older family heads, who had seen the former temple, wept aloud when they saw the foundation of this temple being laid.' It simply wasn't as good as they remembered it from the old days. It was gingernuts; it was mini-discs! It was not what nostalgia had led them to expect; it was just a functional building. They were right, because the rebuilt temple was a simple affair, not meant to inspire with its glory, but a place to do business with God. And so with the shouts of joy there were also tears of disappointment, and the Bible tells us that you couldn't tell one from the other.

> Luck lies in not getting what you thought you wanted but getting what you have, which once you have it you may be smart enough to see is what you would have wanted had you known.
>
> Garrison Keillor, novelist, born 1942

Who had the correct response? Both, I think. God understands these emotions, because he is a God of the past and the present and the future. And it is when all those are in balance, looking forward as well as looking back, that the work we do for him is honoured.

Detox: Think back to what you were doing five years ago. Make a list of things that have improved in your life since then (even if they are few). Thank God.

Eternal God, poised at this moment between my past and my future, I ask that I may let go without regret of all that holds me back, and face with enthusiasm the changes that are to come. Amen.

Detox your expectations

Day 22

Hope for the best

My godson has asked for a metal detector for his birthday. Oh dear! Have you any idea how much a metal detector costs? He is desperate, absolutely desperate, to have one. I don't see how I can let him down. Several of us are clubbing together so that we can afford it. He is convinced that there is pirate treasure buried in the woods at Purley. There is no point in explaining that we live 50 miles from the coast, or that pirates sailed on the other side of the Atlantic, because he is so single-minded. I wish I could share his irrepressible hope. Deep down I know that there are no pearls in Purley.

The stories that Jesus told about a hidden treasure and a perfect pearl are about coming to the point when suddenly your priorities are clear. The things that matter really matter. The things that you can either take or leave drop out of the frame.

> Jesus said, 'The kingdom of heaven is like treasure hidden in a field. When a man found it, he hid it again, and then in his joy went and sold all he had and bought that field.'
>
> *Matthew 13.44*

Different things bring people to that point. Sometimes it's an illness that sorts out what is really important to you. Sometimes it's a personal catastrophe or a great loss. But these parables, which are among my favourite parts of the Bible, are not about how disasters bring us to God. They are the complete opposite. They are completely joyful in every way about laying hold of God as a glorious discovery.

DETOX YOUR SPIRITUAL LIFE

There is no sadness in them at all. The man who sells everything he's got and invests it all in one pearl doesn't make a
big deal of it. He doesn't mention the gritted-teeth sacrifice
of losing everything else. He doesn't have a moment's regret
about what he now cannot do because of what he's chosen.
It is all joy: the finding, the selling, the buying, the owning.
Every moment of the process is wonderful. He has suddenly got a life!

> Jesus said, 'The kingdom
> of heaven is like a
> merchant looking for
> fine pearls. When he
> found one of great value,
> he went away and sold
> everything he had and
> bought it.'
>
> Matthew 13.45–46

These parables are about
how to hope for the best –
literally, hope for the best!
They are about the relief of
unburdening yourself of all
that wretched, cluttering, dis-
tracting *stuff* that comes
between us and the best of
treasures. All that gadgetry
which bleeps and lights up and
twiddles and eats up the rain-
forest and shouts out, 'You
must have me! Just look how
much dust I can collect! Dust like mine will thrill your soul!'
The secret these parables give away is that the life which is
really living comes when you find that what you have set
your heart on single-mindedly is one and the same as what
God has in mind for you.

The stories are not quite the same. In the parable of the
pearl, the merchant goes out hunting for what he needs. But
in the parable of the hidden treasure, the farmer stumbles
upon the precious thing quite by accident – in a field that he
had often walked through before when he had completely
other concerns on his mind. And it's true that some people
stumble upon Jesus in a transforming way when it is the last
thing that they expected.

I suppose that happened to me. I was brought up going

to church, never thinking there was a proper alternative. I was dismayed by a tragedy into dropping out of regular worship. I drifted through college vaguely aware that there were some truly ghastly people meeting as a Christian Union. I paid lip-service to saying my prayers until suddenly in my early twenties, not looking for him at all, Jesus took hold of me. It was not the church, the joy of belonging to which I came to a long time

> You called, you cried, you shattered my deafness. You sparkled, you blazed, you drove away my blindness. You shed your fragrance, and I drew in my breath, and I pant for you.
>
> *Augustine, Bishop of Hippo, 354–430*

afterwards. It was not middle-class Christian morality, which I still struggle and fight with many years later. And it was not the disciplines of faith, which I am going to have a battle with until the day I die.

> My brother, may the Son of God who is already formed in you, grow in you so that for you he will become immeasurable, and that in you he will become laughter, exultation, the fullness of joy which no one takes from you.
>
> *Isaac, Abbot of Stella, 1100–69*

No! It was the character of Jesus who reached out and grabbed me and still hasn't let me go, although I've shaken hard enough. The character of the man who, brought up in the artisan middle-classes – educated, intelligent – turned his back on all of that, and made his home among the poor. The man who made himself completely reliant on others, defied convention, stayed single, trod a delicate line between friends in the brothel and friends in the synagogue, inspired people that a world of justice was not only desirable but possible, and died with words of love and forgiveness on his lips. The pearl!

Well, I hope my godson has a heap of fun with his metal detector. You know, if he finds something and proves my scepticism wrong I will be so, so happy. But I have got a hidden agenda to go with his hidden treasure. I am praying that somewhere along the line in the wonderful future of a wonderful little boy (and preferably after he's had an opportunity to fling a small handful of wild oats as far as they can decently go) he stumbles upon Jesus as a treasure of inestimable value. He knows the name; he knows the routine; he's been surrounded by the love of a church all his life. But I'm waiting for the day when, unexpectedly I'm sure, Jesus reaches out and grabs hold of him.

Because then he will find that everything else that was important to him, metal detector and all, can be traded in with much rejoicing as he makes his journey home.

Detox: Looking back on your life, what was the point at which Jesus took hold of you? Were you searching for him, or did you stumble upon him? At what moments in your past have you genuinely treasured the presence of Jesus in your life? How could you rediscover that excitement?

O God, do not remain hidden any longer. Sparkle in the dust of my life until I recognize you to be my greatest treasure. Amen.

Day 23

Check your ambitions

I've just wasted yet another evening because I got hooked on a television programme that counted down the world's best films from 100 to one. Why are we so compelled by lists of the 100 best adverts, or richest people, or strongest brands? Why at the same time do we need to shame the weakest schools or the least effective hospitals? When is it right to want to be best? Would it be a worthy ambition to want to be part of the best church? Or to be the best Christian?

The story of the Tower of Babel is a terrific warning about ambitions. We think the tower was a failure because the people's ambition was too big; in fact, their ambition was too small! Imagining yourself into the story, you can

[People] said, 'Come, let us build ourselves a city, with a tower that reaches to the heavens, so that we may make a name for ourselves and not be scattered over the face of the whole earth.' But the Lord came down to see the city and the tower that they were building. The Lord said, 'If as one people speaking the same language they have begun to do this, then nothing they plan to do will be impossible for them. Come, let us go down and confuse their language so they will not understand each other.' So the Lord scattered them from there over all the earth, and they stopped building the city. That is why it was called Babel.

Genesis 11.3–9

overhear the architects' discussion: 'It's going to be so big that it will reach heaven, and from the top we will rival God.'

But from heaven God looks down and moans, 'Where is this midget thing they are knocking up? It's hopeless, I can't see it. Give me a telescope! Still too tiny! I'll have to go down there and see what all the hullabaloo is about.' And in the end, what has happened to the great Tower of Babel? Rubble! Babble! Squabble! Trouble!

Churches need to learn the lesson of this story because they bring substantial numbers of men and women together, and in any group where people gather they compare themselves. In those circumstances, ambitions come into perspective and success comes to be valued very highly. It is valued in a way that puts intolerable pressure on children who are lovely but not academically brilliant, on women who are gorgeous but not wafer-thin, on men who are profoundly good but not in careers that earn a lot of money, on high fliers who exhaust themselves spiritually in the attempt to be the highest flier, on anyone who cannot look at herself as God sees her because she is only aware of how others see her.

> About your mutual love we do not need to write to you, for you yourselves have been taught by God to love each other ... Make it your ambition to lead a quiet life, to mind your own business and to work with your hands, just as we told you, so that your daily life may win the respect of outsiders and so that you will not be dependent on anybody.
>
> *1 Thessalonians 4.9–12*

At some point in our daily lives we all meet someone who earns a lot and would like to earn more. Or someone who lives in a big house and would like a bigger one. What's wrong with those ambitions? Are they too big? No, the problem with ambitions like those is that they are too small.

Make your ambitions bigger! Don't just build for earth; build for eternity. Build something that lasts longer than the bricks and mortar of Babel. Build the inner life both of yourself and of those around you. Build love between people, because that will last into eternity. Build inner beauty in people, because that will bloom in heaven. Build truth and integrity in people, because they lead directly to God. Build people's spirit, because the human spirit is where we meet the Spirit of God eternally.

The church throughout the world has had a chequered history. Sometimes it has been the most powerful force on the planet; sometimes (as now in the UK) it has been a rather feeble institution. It seems to me that at the times when it was most powerful it was probably at its worst. It was power that sent the Christians to fight the Crusades, attempting to wrest control of the places where Jesus lived from Muslim control, and bringing misery which is still unfolding in

> If you plan to build a high house of virtues, you must first lay deep foundations of humility.
>
> Augustine, Bishop of Hippo, 354–430

the Middle East 700 years later. It was fear of losing power that drove the Inquisition, burning and torturing and terrorizing, to stamp out heresy in the name of God in the fourteenth century.

I have an unconventional view: that the church is doing more good today in its rather puny state than it ever did when it was wealthy and influential. Christians were never meant to wield power; they were meant to model servant-hood. I sometimes find myself singing the song 'There is power in the name of Jesus'. As I sing I think to myself that it is indeed true – the name of Jesus has a phenomenal

> Keep clear of every conference of bishops, for I never saw good come of one. They are more likely to increase evils than remedy them, for ambition gets the upper hand of reason.
>
> *Gregory of Nazianzus, church leader, 330–90*

power. But please God, in your mercy, don't let us get hold of any of it!

In contrast, I regularly see Christian people come alongside friends in their weakness. They talk about what has gone wrong, and pray together about putting it right. They lay out their disappointments, and cry a bit, and hold each other compassionately, and say, 'I need help.' And then others say, 'Well, I need help too! Could we help each other?' People who do that put themselves in a position where weakness is not a shame, but a starting point for God to move in. We need to recognize that as something very precious and godly. Those are the times when people's lives change for the better.

In the Bible Paul seems to recognize this. He was the first great empire builder for the Christian church, but when he suggested what the height of ambition could be for a follower of Jesus the four things he chose were love, quietness, contentment and work. It is entirely typical of the topsy-turvy values of the Kingdom of God that virtues as simple as those are deemed magnificent.

Why are they fine ambitions? Because they have God as their focus. They do not point at yourself; they point at him. Ordinary, unspectacular goodness is the greatest of Christian ambitions. It is building for eternity. God sets before us the monumental follies of ambition, crumbling into rust and dust, or the lasting ambitions of living for something indestructible. What you choose will make all the difference! Don't fritter life away on small ambitions; think as big as heaven!

Detox: Examine the ambitions that are in your mind at the moment – concerning your accommodation, job, transport, education, church, relationships, children, finance. Which of them will have an impact on earth and which in eternity? Which need to increase and which need to be humbled?

Teach me, Lord God, to be jealous of no one, generous to anyone and compassionate to everyone. Amen.

Day 24

Save time

I am trying to devise a new system of technology in which occasionally, just occasionally, a human is allowed to drive a computer to the end of its tether. Wouldn't that feel good! It would be sweet revenge for all the times when that wretched machine has wasted my day and exhausted my energy so utterly. I never used to feel this way about a pencil and paper!

The speed at which we achieve things has become increasingly important as the opportunities to do more and more during one lifetime have opened up. An entire industry has sprung up to help people manage their time wisely so that work, relaxation, relationships and spirituality are all held in balance. Consultants in time management try to help us bring these things together to create people who are making the most of the few decades of our endless lives that we get to spend on this planet. To do that they focus on four things.

First of all they invite us to clarify our personal goals – to line up the specific, achievable tasks toward which we want to work during a certain period of time. It could be a week's plan or a five year plan, but it does help us to be sure what our priorities are so that we can assess whether or not we are achieving worthwhile things.

Second, they ask us to reflect on the way we have used time in the past. Sometimes that means keeping a logbook of where the time goes. It can show us whether time went by because we achieved desirable things, because we were

You were once darkness, but now you are light in the Lord. Live as children of light (for the fruit of the light consists in all goodness, righteousness and truth) and find out what pleases the Lord. Have nothing to do with the fruitless deeds of darkness, but rather expose them. . . . Be very careful, then, how you live – not as unwise but as wise, making the most of every opportunity, because the days are evil. Therefore do not be foolish, but understand what the Lord's will is.

Ephesians 5.8–11, 15–17

wastefully undisciplined, because the needs of other people impinged unexpectedly on ours, and so on. That can prompt decisions about how we can be more in control in the future.

Third, they ask us to think of specific habits and skills we could develop in order to make maximum use of the time. This involves working out the times of day during which we are most wide awake, so that the important things can happen at those times. (And, of course, the important things are not always work – they might be times set aside to pray, or to read stories to children, or to be intimate with a lover.) Skills in communication and organization can be learnt as well, so that we don't waste four e-mails on a situation that could be resolved by one phone call, or spend a frantic evening looking for the car's MOT certificate because every year it gets put in a different place.

And the final thing that time management experts encourage us to do is to develop skills with people. That means practising not speaking when silence would be better for everyone concerned. It might also mean knowing when to seek time alone, as Jesus did. Or being aware of whose company enriches your life and whose is a drain on it. (That does not result in avoiding altogether people who require a lot of support; it means devising ways in which those people do not exhaust your measure of compassion and leave you too paralysed to help others.)

People skills. And valuable habits. And reflection on how you divide up your time. And clarification of your personal goals.

Where did those four things come from? I have no idea! But I can't help noticing that they feature again and again in the advice that Paul gives in his letters to the churches during the years after Jesus' resurrection. 'Live as children of light,' he writes in Ephesians, 'in all goodness, righteousness and truth, and find out what pleases the Lord.' Shine a light on your own life so that you can clarify your goals and see which are driven by godly values. Alongside the goals you want to achieve in your working life, and what you want to devote to your friends and family, shine a light on what you want to be in your spiritual life. For instance, how involved do you want to be in the life of a church? What activity might have to be put aside because of what you feel called to do among your fellow Christians? Of course, it might be the other way round as well! Only shining a light on the question will allow you to answer it in a guilt-free way.

> There is a time for everything, and a season for every activity under heaven.
>
> *Ecclesiastes 3.1*

When it came to asking the church in Ephesus to reflect on how they used and wasted time, Paul wrote: 'Be very careful, then, how you live – not as unwise but as wise,

> Don't imagine that if you had a great deal of time you would spend more of it in prayer. Get rid of that idea! Again and again God gives more in a moment than in a long period of time, for his actions are not measured by time at all.
>
> *Teresa of Avila, nun, 1515–82*

making the most of every opportunity, because the days are evil.' People who do not use their time foolishly, he says, come to understand what the Lord's will is for their life.

It's like playing cricket (which in itself is either the most refreshing tonic or the biggest waste of time, depending on your attitude). Suppose each hour is a cricket ball. As you stand, bat in hand, it is hurtling towards you with evil intent – to bowl you out middle stump. Your task is to play each ball wisely, so that you turn the potential evil of being caught into the great good of smashing the ball over the boundary.

> Do not walk through time without leaving worthy evidence of your passage.
> *John XXIII, pope, 1881–1963*

Don't fritter away opportunities or bad light will stop play!

What would you like to do more of? Don't pray for more time to do it; pray for more heart to do it. And ask the Lord of light to show you the next step to achieving it.

Detox: For the next seven days, which is 168 hours, keep a record of precisely how you allocate your time. On a piece of paper create a chart that is divided into 15-minute intervals, and record what you are doing. At the end of the week add up the time spent in various categories: sleep, eating, travel, work, prayer, television, housework, with friends and with family, and so on. Think about whether you are content with what has been revealed, and consider whether it is possible to make changes.

God of every passing moment, take away the waste that comes when I should be doing something more productive. And take away the guilt that comes when I shouldn't! Amen.

Day 25

Make a sacrifice

There are stories in the Bible that I love and others that I find chilling. But there is one that many people loathe. In it God tells an old man to kill his son. Abraham takes Isaac, born in old age, to the top of a mountain. He binds him and raises his knife, ready to make the human sacrifice that God demands of him. Then, when the (superbly told) story is at a pitch of excitement, God halts Abraham. Isaac is spared and a ram is sacrificed instead.

What kind of God asks a father to kill his son? It's a story that has come down to us from barbaric times. But it is easy to misunderstand, because we don't realize what the society in which Abraham lived was like. His neighbours believed in hundreds of gods, each with their own idol, whom they tried to avoid angering. In that setting, Abraham must have seemed to be going mad because he believed two things: that there was only one real God, and that God was invisible.

> By faith Abraham, when God tested him, offered Isaac as a sacrifice. He who had received the promises was about to sacrifice his one and only son . . . Abraham reasoned that God could raise the dead, and figuratively speaking, he did receive Isaac back from death.
>
> Hebrews 11.17, 19

Once you know that, the story seems different. God tells Abraham to worship. That's no surprise, it's what all the so-called gods of the time ask. God requires a mountain-top sacrifice. That's no surprise either – all the gods require that. God demands that Abraham kill his first-born child. In those dark days, that too is what everyone expects of their gods.

It is only then that the real shock of the story comes. As the father lifts the knife, God yells, 'Stop!' Now Abraham really is surprised, and the audience who first heard the story would have been too. Abraham's God, the only true God, is different. He utterly abhors the sacrifice of children. The Old Testament repeatedly tells us that is so. Nowadays, we are shocked that God leads someone to the point of child abuse, but the storyteller originally meant us to be shocked that God doesn't demand such a sacrifice. He would never inflict such misery on the humans whom he loves. It is something he could only ask of himself!

What Abraham was not required to do for God, God freely did for humankind! When Jesus died on a hill outside the city walls, not far from Moriah where Abraham's story is set, it provided once and for all everything that was required to reconcile humans to God. It was a sacrifice. Blood was shed so that sins could be forgiven. And that is why blood will never have to be shed again in order to please the Lord. Not from us, not from our children, not from anyone. That is the gift of God, and that is the Christian faith.

And yet! And yet in a way God asks us for more than a son. He asks us to risk everything for him. He says to us, 'Because you trust me, dare everything! Defy the world's standards and do what is good. Love in a different way. Spend

> I urge you, brothers and sisters, in view of God's mercy, to offer yourselves as living sacrifices, holy and pleasing to God – this is your spiritual act of worship. Do not conform any longer to the pattern of this world, but be transformed by the renewing of your mind.
>
> *Romans 12.1*

in a different way. Care in a different way. Prioritize in a different way – a total sacrifice.' Real faith means obediently trusting God when the things he is putting us through seem as testing, awful and undeserved as the loss of a child.

The challenge of the story of Abraham and Isaac is the challenge of a bacon and egg breakfast. A chicken and a pig both contribute to making breakfast. For the chicken it's a gift, but for the pig it's a sacrifice!

The way we set our priorities divides us into chicken or pig Christians. Chicken Christians spend their money on necessities and luxuries throughout the month, and at the end of it they spare what's left to give to God's work. Pig Christians decide at the beginning of the month that every penny they have is going to be God's and then work out how he would like them to spend it, pound by pound, decision by decision.

Chicken Christians work out each week whether they can spare time to worship, to be neighbourly, to bring good news to the poor. Pig Christians know from the very first moment of the week that all their time is God's. They are open for him to tell them how to use it – in prayer, in Christian service, and (because that is the nature of our loving God) sometimes just in frivolity.

> Jesus Christ, the only Son of God, is my God. Beat, tear or burn me, and if my words offend you, cut out my tongue. Every single part of me is ready when God calls for it as a sacrifice.
>
> *Theodore of Heraclea, martyr, circa 290–319*

But here is an irony! It is those that surrender most sacrificially who discover true blessing from God. Those who come before him with completely empty hands know that what is placed in them is provided by him and him alone. When the ghastly episode was over, Abraham gave a name to the place where his son faced death. He called it 'The Lord will provide'. Its name has changed often down the centuries. Today we know it as Jerusalem. What a powerful sign of an old man's faith that he came through such a difficult time and was able to say at the end of it, 'This is what I have learnt – the Lord will provide.'

So the story has a happy ending. It would be easy to assume that all the stories are supposed to have happy endings. But no Christian experiences that, and, actually, neither did Abraham. From that day forward he had a habit of breaking into tears. And his relationship with his son Isaac was never close. The scars of what happens in your childhood do not go away that simply.

I hope I never have to face what Abraham faced. But if I do I hope I will find, like him, that God is compassionate, that he is trustworthy, that he will provide. Because to find that is to lay hold of life!

> Take, Lord, and receive all my liberty, my memory, my understanding, and my entire will – all that I have and possess. Thou hast given it all to me. To thee, O Lord, I return it. All is thine, dispose of it wholly according to thy will. Give me thy love and thy grace, for this is sufficient for me.
>
> *Ignatius of Loyola, founder of the Jesuits, 1491–1556*

Detox: Look ahead to the end of this 40 day detox. Make plans now about what you will dedicate to God during that period – in worship, in time and in money. Set those things aside now, so that all your other needs and luxuries fit in what you have spare. Can you make a habit of operating in this way?

Lord God, without you I have nothing. Accept what I offer willingly. Change my heart over what I offer unwillingly. And, in your mercy, forgive what I cannot let go of. Amen.

Day 26

Rejuvenate

It's all falling apart!

My back is aching as if a sumo wrestler mistook me for a floor cushion. On Wednesday I broke a tooth on an extra large peanut. I had gone deaf in one ear even before Paul arrived in my house with his taste for skater punk. And how on earth does God think he has progressed human evolution by taking the hair off my head and putting it in my ears?

The doctor tells me I am suffering from being 45 in a soul that wants to be 20. The final straw is that Paul, who really is 20, has started telling me with exaggeratedly loud precision, 'Don't worry, nurse will be here soon. She'll take you out for a nice walk. Wrap up warm!'

I need what Paul discovered (the one in the Bible, not the

> We have this treasure in jars of clay to show that this all-surpassing power is from God and not from us. We are hard pressed on every side, but not crushed; perplexed, but not in despair; persecuted, but not abandoned; struck down, but not destroyed. . . . Therefore we do not lose heart. Though outwardly we are wasting away, yet inwardly we are being renewed day by day. For our light and momentary troubles are achieving for us an eternal glory that far outweighs them all. So we fix our eyes not on what is seen, but on what is unseen. For what is seen is temporary, but what is unseen is eternal.
>
> *2 Corinthians 4.7–9, 16–18*

one in the guest room). How did he manage to stay so relentlessly optimistic when he was 'hard pressed on every side, but not crushed; perplexed, but not in despair'?

When he felt as fragile as 'jars of clay', he was able to rely on the power of God. One of the difficulties of thinking about power is that we tend to associate it with B-52 bombers. When reporters say that warplanes are powerful they mean that they blast problems away with shock and awe. So we expect the power of God to manifest itself with great miracles. But Paul tells us that scraping through by the skin of our teeth is also the resurrection power of God. 'Persecuted, but not abandoned; struck down, but not destroyed,' does not lead us to expect a jubilant triumph, but to breathe a sigh of relief and lurch on with a battered handful of faith.

Paul encourages us to glimpse eternity whenever we begin to feel old: 'Though outwardly we are wasting away, yet inwardly we are being renewed day by day.' The concept of being renewed takes some getting used to because it defies all logic! Although your physical body started young and is growing older, your spiritual life is making its journey on earth backwards. Your soul started life old, and it is becoming younger and younger. One day, when all the aches and pains catch up with you and you die, your spiritual self will have worked its way back to day one. And then to zero. And then you'll be born again into God's presence, fresh and perfect and full of potential.

As troubles age our outside, they are rejuvenating our spiritual lives as part of the process that God puts us through to get us to heaven. So I have no need to put up with young Paul's 'poor old man' jibes any longer. His inner life is in the Post Office queue drawing its pension; my inner life has changed into its Tommy Hilfiger and is on its way to the nightclub.

How do you take advantage of this brilliant discovery

> We know that if the earthly tent we live in is destroyed, we have a building from God, an eternal house in heaven, not built by human hands. Meanwhile we groan, longing to be clothed with our heavenly dwelling, because when we are clothed, we will not be found naked. For while we are in this tent, we groan and are burdened, because we do not wish to be unclothed but to be clothed with our heavenly dwelling, so that what is mortal may be swallowed up by life.
>
> *2 Corinthians 5.1–4*

when what you see, tough times and bruised bodies, is at odds with what God wants you to see? 'Fix your eyes not on what is seen, but on what is unseen. For what is seen is temporary, but what is unseen is eternal.' In God's great plan for his people, weakness is part of the preparation for being forever strong.

Our true home, the one for which we have been intended right from the start of time, is elsewhere. It is with God in heaven. No wonder we feel ill at ease sometimes here on earth! We are wearing all the wrong clothes. We are dressed for camping out in a tent, when in fact God has destined us for a palace. Of course that makes us feel inadequate! When you are in your gumboots trudging across a field in the middle of the night to get to the toilet in the sluicing rain, and you've just tripped over a guy rope and dropped your torch in the mud, someone inevitably says, 'Are you sure you wouldn't rather be in the

> Age is not all decay; it is the ripening, the swelling, of the fresh life within, that withers and bursts the husk . . . When we are out of sympathy with the young, then I think our work in this world is over.
>
> *George MacDonald, novelist, 1824–1905*

> Strike that thick cloud of unknowing with the sharp dart of longing love, and on no account whatever think of giving up.
>
> The Cloud of Unknowing, *an anonymous book of spiritual reflections, circa 1370*

Hilton Hotel?' Well obviously you'd rather be in the Hilton Hotel – you're just not dressed for it! 'While we are in this tent, we groan and are burdened, because we do not wish to be unclothed but to be clothed with our heavenly dwelling.'

What we cling to in those circumstances is our guarantee that we are heading for the place where everything that diminishes us – sadness, weakness, failure – will be completely taken over by life. Real life! Total life!

How can you be strong when you feel like death? Struggle on. Keep your eyes on your true home. Grow younger and younger until you are ready for God to pick you up in his arms.

It's all falling back together again!

Detox: Treat yourself to something that is going to make you feel younger. Depending on your circumstances it might be something to freshen your appearance – a haircut or something new to wear. Or it might involve some sport or exercise. Or perhaps make time for something you used to enjoy but have not had time for in recent years. As you do so, think about what you have gained and lost with passing time, and enjoy the prospect of being forever young in the eternity you will spend in God's company.

Lord God, turn my times of weakness into times of trust, so that every passing year may be one in which I rejoice in all that is good about my age. Amen.

Day 27

Think about death

The average life expectancy of someone in the UK is 77. In Sierra Leone it is 36. People who live close to death develop an attitude to it which is far more balanced than ours. That is not to say that people in Sierra Leone don't feel tragedy – the death of a child is an appalling sorrow to bear in the dust of Africa just as it is in a British hospital ward. But thinking often about death gives people a sense of proportion.

In Old Testament times there was no assured belief in life after death. There was a concept of a place of shadows and murk called Sheol which awaited humans, but it was nothing to look forward to. By Jesus' time there was uncertainty, with some Jews believing in a resurrection and others believing that death was final.

Today it seems morbid to say, 'Consider your death carefully and often.' We pay funeral directors and solicitors to

---

[Jesus said, 'Those who experience] the resurrection from the dead will neither marry nor be given in marriage, and they can no longer die; for they are like the angels. They are God's children, since they are children of the resurrection. . . . Even Moses showed that the dead rise, for he calls the Lord "the God of Abraham, and the God of Isaac, and the God of Jacob". He is not the God of the dead, but of the living, for to him all are alive.'

Luke 20.35–38

---

do that in the hope that we never have to see a dead body. We are encouraged instead to think carefully and often about finance, beauty and holidays. Occasional fears come to us all. Even those of us with a Christian faith cannot pretend to know for sure that there is a life after death, because it is impossible to know anything like that without doubts.

I can readily tell you what I don't believe! I don't believe in ghosts. I don't believe in seances that put you in touch with spirits. I don't believe I'm reincarnated and in a previous life I was Cleopatra's cat. I don't believe that my days are numbered by some astrological prediction or the length of a wrinkle on my palm. In fact, I don't believe there is anything at all to be scared of about the mystery of what lies beyond life. I have no patience with any of that twaddle, which has duped money out of so many desperate people.

> The saying that is written will come true: 'Death has been swallowed up in victory.' Where, O death, is your victory? Where, O death, is your sting?
>
> I Corinthians 15.54–55

However, I have come to the conclusion that I am probably going to meet God after I die, and will once again meet the people I have loved. Why? Three reasons!

The first is that Jesus believed in eternal life, and I trust him. In fact, he taunted the Jews who did not share that belief – the Sadducees. They came to him with a devious question devised to get him into a theological mess, but he lunged back. 'Do you believe in the God of Abraham, Isaac and Jacob?' he demanded, to which of course their answer was yes. 'Well he declared himself to be the God of the living, and Abraham, Isaac and Jacob are alive with him right now!' Luke tells us that his opponents were astonished and silenced. Jesus faced death reluctantly and with ferocious doubts, but resolved that he could submit to what was ahead with trust in the God who brings life out of death. I find myself persuaded to share his trust.

The second reason is that something unprecedented happened on the third day after Jesus died. I can't be sure what happened because even the original witnesses weren't sure. They described the Jesus whom they saw after his death as both a real presence and as a vision that came and went. He was both a human figure and something utterly different. He was worshipped by some, while others literally couldn't believe their eyes. But whatever it was, something had reached back to them from beyond the grave and transformed the lives of those left behind in a way that was entirely good and empowering. It was a resurrection.

> It's good to have to think about death. Death is what's real in life. It's just that we find ways to be busy. If we lived every day with death, we would live a different life and it wouldn't necessarily be a depressing one. It would probably be more joyful. I often lose the ability to prioritise. I'm rushing to get lunch for the children, and put the toilet paper on the toilet paper thing, and read the scripts, and it takes a kid getting sick or something to remember that it's not so important that there's stuff all over the floor and maybe, just maybe, you should play with your kids. People say that if we think about death all the time we'd go mad, but maybe we'd go sane.
>
> Susan Sarandon, actress, born 1946

There is one incontrovertible piece of evidence. We go to church on a Sunday. Simple as that! After many centuries during which the people of God were in the habit of worshipping on the last day of the week, something so astonishing happened that instantly the people of God began to worship on the first day of the week. They still do to this day. Something changed on earth because something changed in heaven.

And the third reason is that almost immediately after Jesus ascended, his followers were dying, comforted and without fear, in the knowledge that they were going to a place where they would meet him again. Christian grave-stones that have survived from AD 80 show the engraved image of a shepherd carrying a sheep and the names of believers who, so soon after Jesus had walked the earth, were going to their death in the quiet assurance that they were being carried home.

Among Christians in Sierra Leone, where death is close and each day is a struggle against poverty, there is glorious certainty of an eternity of joy, with hunger and sickness banished, and justice restored. Surely that must be what allows some of them to live such balanced lives, the priori-ties of which we can only envy.

Death is a great leveller and bringer of justice, but if death had the last word we could never be completely fulfilled. Death doesn't have the last word. Death has the last word but one. God is planning to have the last word himself. I don't believe that lightly or without wavering, but I do feel able confidently to let go of friends whom I will

> When it comes time to die, make sure that all you have to do is die.
>
> *Jim Elliot, martyred missionary to the Auca people, 1927–56*

not see on earth again. The Christian faith holds that the last word is actually going to be 'hello'.

Detox: Think about what would need to be done if you were to die tomorrow. Organize yourself today – get your will and papers in order, apologize for things that need to be resolved, complete half-finished tasks, and tell your friends you love them. Then sit back and enjoy every good thing that happens between now and the end of your detox as a glorious bonus of being alive!

Lord Jesus, who has known death, take away my fear and give me instead a love of life and a shining hope. Amen.

Detox your relationships

Day 28

Appreciate friends

Yes, but was the fifth series as good as the legendary second series? This was the main topic of conversation as I was drinking cappuccinos with my friends last night. We were in a coffee shop not unlike the one in the television series *Friends*, and I dared to suggest: 'Yes, but is there any one of the six who you would actually want as a friend in real life?' This categorized me immediately as a nonbeliever and I was shut out of the conversation for an hour!

If it is possible to have that level of interest in the lives of fictional characters, it makes me wonder whether 'friend' has got any meaning left. This morning I added up that I am a friend to six different cultural organizations. I know I am, because I pay my money every year and get priority booking. I'm a friend of the Royal Court Theatre, I'm a friend of the National Gallery, and four others. But there's not much friendship involved in writing the cheque.

And on top of it all, I had junk mail yesterday from an animal sanctuary which said, 'What Charlie the donkey needs is a friend. Will you be that friend?' Well, only if he buys me a cappuccino!

Friendship is an unpredictable relationship. It has no legal standing like a marriage, it has no natural obligations like a parent and child. Some people use it to describe the closest relationship in their life; others to describe someone they don't really like who happens to share an interest or meeting place. It has no specified beginning, because it grows from nothing. And it has no definite end, because even if there has been a row there is nothing to lose should you decide to give it another go. Friends make up their own rules each time.

I am not sure what detoxing your friendships will involve in practice, but I am hoping that it will not involve altering the contact you have with particular people. Rather, I hope it will increase the value that those relationships give to your life.

> Wounds from a friend can be trusted, but an enemy multiplies kisses ... Perfume and incense bring joy to the heart, and the pleasantness of one's friends springs from their earnest counsel. Do not forsake your friend ... when disaster strikes you, better a neighbour nearby than a relative far away.
>
> *Proverbs 27.6, 9, 10*

The Bible invariably refers to friendship as something good. It teaches us that friends are worth having – not just acquaintances, but friends. People make acquaintances for all sorts of reasons: because they feel they can benefit, because it makes them look good, because they feel sorry for someone, sometimes because there is no one else around! But the most famous friendship in the Bible was not like that. Jonathan and David (whose family circumstances might have made them enemies) found themselves 'one in spirit'. That is the difference, I think, between an easy-come-easy-go acquaintance and a true friend.

David might have been a threat to Jonathan, because he had stolen his position as the national military hero. The public would always admire Jonathan, but he knew they

> Jonathan said to David, 'Go in peace, for we have sworn friendship with each other in the name of the Lord, saying, "The Lord is witness between you and me ... for ever".'
>
> *1 Samuel 20.42*

What though the roads and mountains and the sea between us are, that which no earth can hold still follows thee . . . Christ, who first gave thee as a friend to me, keep thee well, where'er thou art. Earth's self shall go and the swift wheel of heaven perish and pass, before our love shall cease. Do but remember me, as I do thee, and God, who brought us on this earth together, bring us together in his house of heaven.

Hrabanus Maurus, Archbishop of Mainz, Germany, 788–856, to his friend Grimold, who was Abbot of St Gall

would worship David. A rivalry of celebrities is measured today by the number of appearances in tabloid newspapers, but in 1000 BC it was a matter of who got the most hysterical women out dancing in the streets. David won hands down, but Jonathan was able to enjoy David's success. That's rare, and it is a touchstone of real friendship. The usual attitude is as the novelist Gore Vidal said: 'Whenever a friend succeeds, a little something within me dies.'

Sacrificially to befriend those who need company is always a good thing, but that should not detract from the specialness of developing close, lasting friendships of shared loyalty. One of the Bible's proverbs calls that kind of relationship 'a friend who sticks closer than a brother'. It's different from a family tie or a sexual relationship, but it can give us support, self-esteem, constancy when things change, an honest and listening ear, even accountability. Those things strengthen the joy we take in being single, or in our family life, or in our ability to be pure sexually, or in all three! We all benefit from friends, whether we are single or married, living alone or living with a family. If you assume that there is no room in your life for friends because your partner or your family take their place, you will lose out in the long run. And yes, Proverbs tells us that as well.

Don't settle for friendliness when you need friendship –

why order spam when you really want steak! Friendliness arrives with a take-it-or-leave-it attitude to people; friendship attracts the kind of generosity, honesty and trust that Jonathan and David risked to create a relationship the value of which is still talked of 3,000 years later. It may be that one of the ways of developing it was their shared commitment to recognizing the place of God in their lives – the fact that 'the Lord was witness' between them. I am not suggesting, of course, that friendship can only be valuable between people of the same religion, but there is something priceless about a friendship in which God is spoken of in an unforced way. It brings a deep mutual understanding of the context for the advice or help you give each other. Sharing the part God plays in your life might be the beginning of a friendship, or it may be the thing that deepens it much later, but either way it is one of the secrets of making friendships that last. In the case of David and Jonathan, it allowed their relationship to continue enriching their lives despite being forced apart by circumstances, having differences of opinion and, finally, facing death itself.

If ever there was a Christian discipline that repaid the effort it requires in an obvious and happy way, it is the discipline of making friends. Don't overlook it! Put real names against the things you have been thinking as you read this chapter, and then do something practical about it. Nothing is more immediately likely to improve the quality of your life than genuine friendship. And the best of it is, God invented it!

> I have lost friends –
> some by death, others
> through sheer inability
> to cross the street.
> *Virginia Woolf, novelist,*
> *1882–1941*

Detox: Get out your address book!

O God, make me a loyal friend, and give me a loyal friend, so that love and trust may increase in the world. Amen.

Day 29

Meet other Christians

One of my memories of the house in which I grew up is lying in bed, waiting to fall asleep, listening to a rumbling, tumbling, clattering noise rising faintly from the garage that was below my bedroom. My father had taken up stone-polishing as a hobby. He used to collect pebbles and put them in a plastic barrel about the size of a roll of kitchen towel, along with some water and a handful of grit. The barrel rotated on a roller so that the stones bashed and banged against each other for six months in the muddy water. They came out shining like jewels. As a child I can recall hunting on the beach or in the park for promising stones, looking not at the ugly exterior but imagining the jewel inside.

> Let us consider how we may spur one another on towards love and good deeds. Let us not give up meeting together, as some are in the habit of doing, but let us encourage one another – and all the more as you see the Day approaching.
>
> *Hebrews 10.24, 25*

This strikes me as a fine metaphor to explain why God has not left us to struggle on as Christians by ourselves, but has called us together in groups and congregations. Churches always have been and always will be places where we get battered about a bit. That is not because they are imperfect; it is what God always knew would happen. It is because we rub and rattle alongside other Christians, agreeing and disagreeing, enjoying and enraging, but staying together as a worshipping community, that God can smooth out our sharp edges and make us people who gleam.

When we come together to worship in a church or in a similar group of Christian people, we are surrounded by men, women and children who are going through all the various phases of a loving relationship with God. Some are on a besotted first date, while others have exhausted themselves into a weary old trudge. We need to have both these extremes, and every stage of spiritual progress between them, because it is easier to encapsulate honestly what one wants to say to God when one is surrounded by a variety of experiences. Those who are on fire encourage those who are tired. Those who are struggling or in pain keep earthed in reality those who are away on a trip with the angels.

I am very often asked whether it is possible to be a Christian without going to church. It is very tempting to attempt this, because it side-steps the awkward truth that some Christians are hypocritical, some have preferences about the way they express their faith which seem strange, and some are (let's be honest!) downright unpleasant. So is it possible? Yes, of course it is! But if you do so you are missing out on almost all the benefits of being a believer. The church is there to be a community of support and encouragement, a precious resource for people who need help in times of struggle. But the church is also there to be a community of

> [Jesus said to his followers,] 'I am the vine; you are the branches. If you remain in me and I in you, you will bear much fruit; apart from me you can do nothing. If you do not remain in me, you are like a branch that is thrown away and withers.'
>
> John 15.5, 6

struggle and hotchpotch, an underrated resource for people who need realism in times of success.

The writer of the letter to the Hebrews urged his readers not to give up meeting together, even though it felt like hard work. His objective was that love and good deeds should flourish. Neither of those things can happen in isolation; they only happen in a community. And they are proved to be worthwhile when they have a cost attached to them.

When Jesus was looking for a metaphor to describe how something that can appear wounding can in fact be life-enhancing, he did not choose stones, but grapes. The image of a vine, which would have been very familiar to his disciples, is one that speaks of complete connectedness. Every part of such a large plant – roots, shoots and fruits – requires every other part. Jesus was saying, 'You are no use whatever without me. I am no use without you. And you all need each other!' Grapes that cluster together get picked and trodden on. They are crushed and squashed. They are processed and left. But, in time, they become glorious, bubbling champagne.

A gardener does not leave a bush to grow by itself, but will prune it, cutting away parts. It is vicious, but it makes the plant grow stronger. And the cutting, stinging life experiences that we have all experienced are the pruning through which God makes our attachment to Jesus and our support of our fellow humans stronger.

> Let him who cannot be alone beware of community. Let him who is not in community beware of being alone.
>
> *Dietrich Bonhoeffer, theologian, 1904–45*

That is why we need to gather together with other believers. If you sit with a group of Christians and ask them what they have learnt about God they rarely refer to sermons or books, but they often tell of the experiences and people who have left a mark on them. God's mark! And very often it is painful experiences of which they speak – the ideal jobs they didn't get; the friendships that didn't turn into what they wanted; the losses that seemed irreplaceable.

These are the events that shape us into the people God wants us to be. They tumble or crush us. Alone, they might overcome us; in the company of those who are connected to Jesus, they show us how to live worthwhile lives, how to sparkle!

Keep meeting with other Christians – not in spite of the buffeting it may entail, but because of it. Learn, apologize, advise, encourage, fail, admire, dislike, share, help and recover! And emerge from it a jewel fit to present to Jesus! A fine and fizzing new wine!

> Meet together in common – every single one of you – in grace, in one faith, and in one Jesus Christ. For when you meet frequently the forces of Satan are annulled and his destructive power is cancelled as you seek harmony in your faith.
>
> *Ignatius, Bishop of Antioch, circa 50–107*

Detox: Talk to God honestly about the Christians whom you find disagreeable or boring, and ask him to help you find ways of appreciating them. Acknowledge that you have been put together for a purpose, and try to identify how their presence in your life can improve you as a follower of Jesus. Next time you are in a Christian congregation imagine that everyone is a stone bumping against each other, and try to see the jewel within that Jesus sees.

Forgive me, Lord God, for all the times when I have been irritated by people who are precious to you. And forgive me even more when I have been the reason others have been bruised. Amen.

Day 30

Develop a family likeness

Six words I remember from my youth which could totally ruin a day! Aged aunts would come bearing gifts, make a fuss of me, prattle on in an entirely tolerable way – and then those six monosyllables! Clergy would visit the home, say all the usual complimentary words – and then add those wretched six. They are the words a male teenager least wants to hear: 'You are so like your dad!'

Instant dejection! How could anyone growing up in the 1970s (or any other decade for that matter) possibly want to be like his father? What could be less groovy than being compared with someone who has absolutely no concept of the virtues of the music of Marc Bolan and T Rex, or flared trousers, and worst of all, does not realize the vital importance of keeping a full head of hair?

When you are a teenage boy it is a terrible thing to be a son! It's the parents who are the problem! Because of their size parents are very difficult to discipline! You go to a cousin's wedding with an absolute promise that they will be

---

Those who are led by the Spirit of God are children of God. For you did not receive a spirit that makes you a slave again to fear, but you received the Spirit of adoption. And by him we cry, 'Father.' The Spirit himself testifies that we are God's children. Now if we are children, then we are heirs . . . co-heirs with Christ.

Romans 8.14–17

---

on their best behaviour, and then you are confronted with the hideous sight of your father discoing on the dance floor: 'Hey-hey, I haven't lost it yet, lad!' (He is the only person dancing.) 'Why aren't you joining me? I thought you liked this kind of thing.' (His feet are moving in a vague approximation of a slow waltz; his middle-age spread is dancing a quickstep.) 'This is better than the rubbish you listen to – Brontosaurus, or glum rock, or junk, or whatever it's called.'

It is time to excuse yourself and head for the toilet for at least an hour. There you find yourself reflecting on how parents never fulfil the promise of their early years. And you become convinced that you must be the victim of some maternity hospital muddle-up. You are actually, unbeknown to anybody, the child of some really glamorous couple who will claim you as their long-lost son and spirit you away – maybe John Lennon and Yoko Ono, or Terence Stamp and Julie Christie. Witnesses will appear and testify, 'It was all a mistake! He belongs to someone different altogether. Take him away from this slavery and give him what he really deserves.'

'The Spirit himself testifies that we are God's children.' That's what it means to be a Christian. It means being adopted into a family that is different altogether. It is a family in which God answers to the name Father. It is a family in which Jesus stands alongside us as a brother. It is a family in which the Holy Spirit appears as a witness, saying over and over again, 'Don't worry any more. You're safe here. You are God's child and

> The Lord is the Spirit, and where the Spirit of the Lord is, there is freedom. And we, who with unveiled faces all reflect the Lord's glory, are being transformed into his likeness with ever-increasing glory.
>
> 2 Corinthians 3.17–18

no one will ever come between you and him. And there is an unimaginably glorious future to which you are the heir. Believe me!'

That is the life!

How can we have a life like that? How can we become children of God? In his letter to the Christians who lived in Rome, Paul spelled it out: 'Those who are led by the Spirit of God are children of God.' In the society in which he lived only male children could inherit a parent's fortune. Not so God's Paradise! The Kingdom of God was opening up rights to women and men alike, to slaves and free people alike, the like of which they could not even dream in ordinary life. And the way to receive it? By being led by the Spirit of God.

So where does the Spirit of God lead us? Into good things; always and only into good things. For a start, the Spirit leads us into confessing and being rid of what is wrong in our lives. Not because we are fearful of what God will do if we are caught – that's slavery. And Paul makes it clear that, with the Spirit of God, we will never be 'a slave again to fear'. Rather, we find forgiveness for what we have done wrong and make changes in the way we behave because in this good, new family we have a growing desire to be as good as the parent who has adopted us.

It doesn't come right at the beginning. At least, it may do so for some people, but it didn't for me. For me it is something that has grown through the years as I have learnt to be led by the Spirit. The more the Spirit teaches me, the more I can see the goodness of goodness!

> All people are made in God's image; but to be in his likeness is granted only to those who through great love have brought their own freedom into subjection to God.
>
> *Diodochos, Bishop of Photiki, Greece, 400–86*

As God my Father announced himself to the world as good news for the poor, so I want to be creating a world in which the bleak, wretched grind of poverty is done away with. As God my Father announced himself as the one who binds up the broken-hearted, so I want to create a home which weary people find to be a place where their load is lightened. As God my Father revealed himself in gracious, uncompromising love, so I want to have a life in which the love I have for people doesn't depend on what they are giving back, but is generous and open and allows them to grow into the kinds of people God sees them to be.

And now I am about to write something that I could never have said as a teenage boy, but have found out as a Christian man. In this new adopted family, the good family of God, I have found myself wanting to be like God is. I want people to say those six horrendous words – 'You are so like your Father'.

> To be like Christ is to be a Christian.
>
> *William Penn, Quaker and founder of Pennsylvania as a place of religious liberty, 1644–1718*

Detox: Who are the people who have shaped your life in a way that is positive and good? It may be a parent but (for a hundred different reasons) it might be someone completely different whose likeness you see in yourself. Are they aware of your gratitude for what they have done for you? Do you see anything good in yourself that has grown between the first time you were aware of God at work in your life and today? Is God aware of your gratitude that you are becoming like him?

Good Father, so that I may grow more and more like you, drive away from me the fear of fear, and convince me of the goodness of goodness. Amen.

Day 31

Be different

'I acted differently because I honoured God.'

I've known those words almost all my life. Learning verses from the Bible figured strongly in my experience of church as a child. Most of the words I learnt have proved forgettable, but those seven have stayed with me. I think that sentence has had more impact on me than any other from the Bible. Remembering that verse at trivial or important moments has stopped me doing some things and prompted me to do others. It once flashed into my head just as I passed the concrete 'honesty box' of an unattended car park on the south coast without putting any money in. Unfortunately, it didn't stop me reversing into the pillar and denting my bumper when I attempted to put it right without the effort of getting out of the car!

For Nehemiah, who originally wrote the words, it was a matter of political integrity. Having been appointed to a powerful job in Jerusalem, he was in a position to accumulate a personal fortune through taxation. It was, after all, what every other leader did. However, he declined that opportunity because he saw his job as serving people, not benefiting from them. He set to work on a policy of relieving the poorest people in the surrounding area of debts that had reduced them to destitution. He could see no integrity in lining his own pockets while their misery increased.

Of course, not many of us are in a position of political influence. We are not the people who set the standards of our society; we are those who are affected by them. Should we accept them as our own standards just because they are now the norm? Or should we draw attention to ourselves by insisting on alternatives? Those of us who are detoxing our ordinary, uneventful lives need to think about how to stand out in a crowd as people whose values are different, better and designed to please someone altogether more important.

Paul wrote a letter to Timothy, a young man for whom he had a particular fondness as he trained him to lead the next generation of Christians. Paul's suggestion for a distinctive lifestyle was that Timothy should make it clear that his decisions were not driven by how much money he could earn from them. Five centuries had gone by since Nehemiah's time, but the problem was precisely the same. And let's be honest, the prevailing values of today's society are still driven by earning and owning in very much the same way. Paul challenged his protégé to have a different set of values in mind when he made his choices: 'righteousness, godliness, faith, love, endurance and gentleness'.

> [Nehemiah wrote:] 'Earlier governors – those preceding me – placed a heavy burden on the people and took forty shekels of silver from them in addition to food and wine. Their assistants also lorded it over the people. But out of reverence for God I did not act like that. Instead, I devoted myself to the work.'
>
> *Nehemiah 5.15–16*

> Some people, eager for money, have wandered from the faith and pierced themselves with many griefs. But you, man of God, flee from all this, and pursue righteousness, godliness, faith, love, endurance and gentleness.
>
> *1 Timothy 6.10–11*

What do they mean in practice? First, they mean that a person of God is not deflected from his standards by peer pressure. When people are young it is often sexual ethics and the abuse of drugs that present the biggest challenge to acting differently. And when people are older the pressing issues are, well, sexual ethics and the abuse of drugs, actually! 'What will they think of me?' is a paralysing motivation when it comes to deciding what is right. 'How can I bring joy to God?' is a liberating alternative. That is what is meant by 'righteousness and godliness'.

> The Church's service and mission in the world is absolutely dependent on its being different from the world; being in the world but not of the world.
>
> Jim Wallis, founder of the Sojourners' Community, born 1948

Second, it means that a person of God is able to restrain himself or herself and keep to the law, even if everyone else is ignoring it. That is not very difficult if the law in question is murder or treason. But it is harder if the law concerns the age at which you can see a film or go into a pub. And it is harder still if you are surrounded by people who routinely pay less tax than they should, cut corners when it comes to fulfilling a business contract, or treat the M6 motorway like Le Mans. This is where Christians need to show the difference that can be made by 'faith and endurance'.

And third, the person of God can stand out by winning respect through humility, not by throwing his or her weight around. People are not impressed by fine words, but by straightforward actions. And that applies to friends, children, colleagues, members of a sports team, everyone! What does it mean to act differently when the conversation turns to gossip about a local scandal? What does it mean to act differently when a referee fails to notice that you have been fouled inches from the penalty area? These are the moments which give concrete meaning to 'love and gentleness'.

> Christians are no different from the rest of mankind. They do not live in cities of their own or have a different language or way of life . . . but the way they live is marvellous and confounds all expectations . . . They have children, but they don't try to get rid of them. They eat with all their neighbours, but they don't sleep with all their neighbours . . . They obey the existing laws, but in their own lives they surpass the laws. They love all people, even though they are persecuted by all people . . . They are poor, but they enrich other people's lives . . . Their existence is on earth, but they are citizens of heaven.
>
> *Mathetes, author of a letter to Diognetus, circa 200*

This chapter started with a politician creating a national taxation policy, and it ends with a thug of a defender aiming for your shins instead of the football. But that is the nature of God's call. He is at work to improve everything in life, from Parliament Square to Saturday afternoon in the park. And the difference each individual Christian makes, whether they are in a government office or face down in the mud, is his means of changing our world.

Detox: Look back on the opportunities you have had since you began this detox to stand out from the values that the rest of the world takes for granted. Think about your relationships, your finances, your work, your leisure, your moods. Is there anything you would do differently next time out of reverence for God?

Lord God, may the love I have for you make a difference to the way I behave. Not just once, but again and again and again and again. Amen.

Day 32

Explore freedom

Duty used to feature prominently in the church in which I grew up. The church warden was head of the Lord's Day Observance Society, an organization campaigning to prevent the character of Sundays being changed by the legalization of shopping and work on that day. Today, of course, I can see virtue in keeping Sunday distinctive, but aged eight all I knew was that there was a newsagent opposite the church which, for 24 hours each week, turned into the repository of all the evil in London because it sold things on the Sabbath. I also knew that ice cream tasted its sin-flavoured best when you bought it furtively after a church service and ate it hiding behind the church hall, having decided who would be the lookout by drawing lots. So, not only Sabbath abuse, but gambling as well – oh happy days!

I have a different approach these days. I try to persuade children what a special day Sunday is by buying them ice creams twice the usual size.

The Sabbath was given by God so that on one precious day of the week some of us could be set free from having to do paid work. The point of a day of rest is that you find yourself saying, 'Day off! Praise the Lord!' And you can then improve it by doing the praising of the Lord together in the same building. The hope is that if your friends are there, the music is rip-roaring, and what the preacher says is interesting, it will be the highlight of the week. How miserable it would be if this thing that was given to set us free turned into a duty we all feel forced to go through for fear of angering God!

Miserable, yes, but easy to do! It was one of the difficulties the Pharisees got themselves into in Jesus' time. Fervently committed to obeying religious laws, they had allowed their lives to be imprisoned by a faith that was designed to free them. Aghast to see Jesus walking through cornfields picking ears of corn as a snack, they accused him and his disciples of working on the Sabbath. And technically they were – harvesting, grinding, winnowing! If buying ice cream on a Sunday counts as work, then rubbing and nibbling corn does too. I suspect, however, that the Pharisees' real objection was that Jesus and his disciples were enjoying themselves, blissful with God's freedom.

> One Sabbath Jesus was going through the cornfields, and as his disciples walked along, they began to pick some ears of corn. The Pharisees said to him, 'Look, why are they doing what is unlawful on the Sabbath?' . . . Then he said to them, 'The Sabbath was made for people, not people for the Sabbath.'
>
> Mark 2.23–7

And now I want to tell you the most important thing I know.

God loves you. He loves you completely and entirely. He will never love you more than he does at this moment. Even if you become a Christian tomorrow he will not love you more than he does today. He can't, because he loves you perfectly already. His love is absolute and has no qualifications attached to it at all.

But this liberating fact does not stop there. The truth is that not only will God never love you more, he will also never love you less. If you don't read your Bible this week he won't love you less. If you don't pray to him tomorrow he won't love you less. If you never go to church again he won't love you less. That is the freedom of worshipping a God who loves with no conditions, the God of grace.

When you realize this, an entirely different set of priorities takes over. You find yourself beguiled by this God who gives so much and asks so little. Captivated! Not captive to the duties, but captivated by the one we worship.

You hear God say, 'I love you completely,' and your heart is thrilled. And he says, 'Do you want to know more?' and of course you do because it's astounding. So he says, 'Well, all you need to know is available, so why don't you read about it?' And you shout out, 'Where, where, where?' and suddenly you're reading the Bible twice a day. Not as a duty but out of fascination!

> It is for freedom that Christ has set us free. Stand firm, then, and do not let yourselves be burdened again by a yoke of slavery.
>
> *Galatians 5.1*

You hear God say, 'I love you totally,' and your spirit is electrified. And he says, 'Is there anyone who you would like to tell?' and of course there is because it's fantastic. So he says, 'Well, there are opportunities to make it known, so why don't you take advantage of them?' And you cry, 'When, when, when?' and suddenly you're running a children's group, or leading a Bible study, or supporting mission. Not as a duty, but as a delight!

> There are two freedoms – the false, where a man is free to do what he likes; the true, where a man is free to do what he ought.
>
> *Charles Kingsley, novelist, 1819–75*

You hear God say, 'I love you perfectly,' and your soul is ablaze. And he says, 'Is there anything I can do to help?' and, of course, there is, because it would be ridiculous to waste that kind of help. So he says, 'Well, I'm listening any time you want to mention what's on your mind!' And you yell, 'How, how, how?' and suddenly you can't help yourself praying, almost every minute, for the needy world and your needy self. And you have walked out into freedom!

What if this concept of unconditional love is too much to cope with? What if you feel that all you have to offer is a disciplined and dutiful collection of religious observances over which you labour week-in week-out? Well, strange as it seems, that is fine as well. You see, in heaven we will meet the disciples who, on occasion, tried so half-heartedly, but whose love shines out of the stories of the Bible. But we need to realize that in heaven we will also meet the Pharisees who, on occasion, tried so hard, but whose love was notably missing in that field of corn. Thank God that our salvation hasn't come as a result of the effort we put in, but as a gift of Jesus, who offered his life that we might be free.

> God forces no one, for love cannot compel.
> God's service, therefore, is a thing of perfect freedom.
>
> *Hans Denk, Christian leader, 1490–1527*

And when you and I meet in heaven in the fullness of time, I would like to suggest that we head straight for whatever is the nearest equivalent to a cornfield that is available to us in the mysteries that lie ahead, and invite Jesus to the party.

Detox: Make plans for next Sunday as a day to do something good, happily and open-heartedly. Choose something that can be done not because duty requires it, but just because the world is better when good people do good things!

Lord Jesus, lead me out into freedom – kindly and cautiously, thoughtfully and lovingly, joyfully and generously – as on that Sunday when life came leaping from the tomb. Amen.

Day 33

Risk being loved

There is a toy lamb that sits next to my bed. Its name is Larry and I have had it since the day I was born. It was a present from colleagues in the office in which my father worked at that time. It is so ragged that I am the only person who knows what species of animal it was once meant to be. It used to be covered with white, fluffy wool and it had a felt daisy in its mouth. However, every single tuft of wool has fallen out. It has been patched repeatedly. And I ate the daisy.

This is the one possession I would run into a burning house to rescue. I value it so highly because it provides an unbroken link back through every stage of my life to my birth. It has become a powerful symbol for me. You see, it has arrived at such a decrepit state because it has been loved so much!

My pitiful toy lamb speaks to me of the value of love far more realistically than any romantic film or Valentine's Day card. It reminds me that for some people love has meant years of unrelenting service, sometimes bringing rich rewards, but sometimes disappointment. For others it has meant devoted sacrifice, sometimes requited fondly, but sometimes thankless. Love is never wasted. It is only people who have loved until they are threadbare who begin to understand what it has cost God to love humankind with an unbroken devotion through every stage of its evolution from its birth.

In the New Testament, John tells us that anyone who has

given or experienced love has begun to know God. Genuine love for another human is something that can only happen because of the existence of God. So is genuine love of a pet or a place or a piece of music. Even those who do not have a committed faith are not hopelessly adrift from God if they have known love, because every expression of love is an insight into the Lord. And he has proved it. Without a hint of market research to see whether there would be a worthwhile return on his investment, God sent his Son among men and women, giving himself to and for them in the most extreme way imaginable.

> Dear friends, let us love one another, for love comes from God. Everyone who loves has been born of God and knows God. Whoever does not love does not know God, because God is love. This is how God showed his love among us: He sent his one and only Son into the world that we might live through him. This is love: not that we loved God, but that he loved us.
>
> *I John 4.7–10*

But now here is something unexpected to think about. It is easier to love than it is to be loved. Is that true? I think it is.

You can grit your teeth and force yourself to love someone. A stroppy teenager, a friendless neighbour, a senile relative, even a God who appears to have dealt with you cruelly – an effort of will can allow you to develop loving attitudes towards all of these. However, when you look down at a body that is past its prime and a spirit that has been bruised by the passing years, it is not always easy to accept that you are loved. It requires trust that the person expressing that love is telling the truth, has your needs and interests close to their heart, and will not let you down in the future. You cannot force yourself to accept any of those

things; you can only abandon yourself to them in the hope
that you will not be disappointed. It is hard enough to do

> Come with me from Lebanon, my bride,
> come with me from Lebanon.
> Descend from the crest of Amana,
> from the top of Senir, the summit of Hermon,
> from the lions' dens and the mountain haunts of the leopards.
> You have stolen my heart, my sister, my bride;
> you have stolen my heart with one glance of your eyes,
> with one jewel of your necklace.
> How delightful is your love!
>
> *Song of Songs 4.8–10*

that with a human into whose eyes you can look for signs of
integrity; with an invisible God who refuses to be told what
to do it can be even tougher. So come with me on a journey!

Come to Edinburgh, which is my favourite city in the
world. As you leave the city you reach a junction at which
you can go either north or south. The road that goes north
leads up into the craggy, bleak scenery of the Highlands.
The road that goes south leads down towards the warm,
green scenery of the Home Counties. I love those roads
because both are spectacular in
their own way.

However, something in our
experience makes us more at
home in our Christianity with
the north road. We expect our
Christian journey to be one of
dour duty and challenge. Lamentations! But the Bible tells us
of a spiritual road that leads
south as well. It is a road of

> In the beginning God
> created humankind,
> not because he needed
> them, but so that he
> might have someone
> on whom to lavish his
> love.
>
> *Irenaeus, Bishop of Lyons,
> 130–202*

contentment and generosity. It shows us God as a bridegroom devoted to the bride. It speaks to us with a language of love. A song of songs! 'Come with me my bride, come with me . . . You have stolen my heart . . . How delightful is your love! How pleasing!'

This is the language of God to his own people. It cuts through the guilt of the past; it cuts through the inadequacy of the present. Sometimes we are waiting to hear God communicate with us with the strict orders of a lord: 'You will do this because I am God and there is no other.' But it is possible that because of this we miss what he is actually saying to us, which is: 'Here is a day. It is full of beauty and potential because I made it. What would you like to do in it? Let's do that together!'

Risk letting God love you. Grow old along with him, recognizing that the batters and bruises you are aware of, visible and invisible, have been acquired as part of a lifetime in which you have been deeply loved. Let go of the need to grind your way through an austere relationship with him, and attempt to hear him calling you into an embrace in which your aches can be tended to. 'Come with me my bride, come with me. How delightful!'

> Some day, after mastering the wind, the waves, the tides and gravity, we shall harness for God the energies of love. And then, for the second time in the history of the world, mankind will discover fire.
>
> *Pierre Teilhard de Chardin, scientist, 1881–1955*

Detox: Every time you see your name written down between now and the end of these 40 days, murmur to yourself, 'Someone loves that person.' Whenever you see it on a work document, letter or a rota, register that God knows your name and loves every wrinkled and imperfect inch of you. Each time, draw a little tick beside your name as a secret acknowledgement.

Dearest God, this is what I plan to do tomorrow and it would give me great joy if you were to come with me as my loving and faithful friend. Amen.

Detox your spiritual life

Day 34

Wonder

I saw the sun rise yesterday. I didn't mean to, but Paul had to start a day's work in a remote village before the trains were operating, so, drowsy and grumbling, I drove him there. The colours on the horizon were so stunning that I stopped the car in a lay-by and watched for ten minutes. It occurred to me that suns are probably rising in majestic colours on planets a million light-years away with no one to see them. Good God! Lucky me!

Isaiah told of a God who is bigger, wiser and more inexplicable than anything we dare imagine. 'Lift your eyes and look to the heavens.' In Babylon, where he may have been living, astronomy was a brand new science and people were staggered by the advances that had been made. The pioneering astronomer Hipparchus had created a map of the night sky and had charted 3,000 stars. Unbelievable! You can imagine the people of the time saying, 'Now we

> Do you not know? Have you not heard?
> Has it not been told you? . . .
> Lift your eyes and look to the heavens:
> Who created all these?
> He who brings out the starry host one by one,
> and calls them each by name.
> Because of his great power and mighty strength,
> not one of them is missing.
>
> Isaiah 40,21, 26

know the full scale of God's creation; now we understand what God has done!' In that setting, where people were sure that they had the measure of God, Isaiah delivered a warning: You have no idea! Don't even presume to imagine you can sum up the mind of God on the basis of what you understand so far.

Time showed Isaiah to be right. In 1610 Galileo invented the telescope and suddenly the scale on which God is working in his cosmos was shown to be quite different from anything that anyone had previously thought. 'Whom did the Lord consult to enlighten him, and who taught him the right way?' asked the prophet. And, obviously, today we realize that Galileo only knew a tiny fraction.

Our generation is, of course, so, so clever! We can look at the stars and tell God what he did in ancient history, and how long ago he did it, and what his plans have been as the world subsequently evolved. In fact, many people look at the stars and announce that there is no need for the existence of God to account for them at all. So great is the cleverness of human development between then and now that we have succeeded in putting a hole in the ozone layer, an achievement that would have staggered Isaiah. And we know we're in trouble, but we don't know how to plug it up again. Somewhere echoing through space and time I can hear Isaiah's voice saying, 'You have no idea, you have no idea! He is bigger. She is wiser. Language breaks down! God is more inexplicable.'

What do you do when you realize that God is a God beyond compare? You stand back in overwhelmed awe and you worship. You become aware that nothing you could say or sing or think comes close to the greatness of God, but you try your best anyway. In Isaiah's day, when the acceptable means of worshipping God was to sacrifice animals by fire, how big an altar should you build in order to express the message that you want to send God? Is one the size of a

The heavens declare the glory of God;
the skies proclaim the work of his hands. . . .
In the heavens he has pitched a tent for the sun,
which is like a bridegroom coming forth from his pavilion,
like a champion rejoicing to run his course.
It rises at one end of the heavens
and makes its circuit to the other;
nothing is hidden from its heat.

Psalm 19.1, 4–6

house sufficient? The size of a city? How many animals do you have to set alight in order to give a sense of how powerful you imagine God to be? Would a zoo-full be sufficient? Nowhere near, gasped Isaiah: 'Lebanon in its entirety is not sufficient for altar fires, nor all its animals enough for burnt offerings.' Good grief!

Terrible things happen in the name of God. Wars are fought and justified in that name. Cultures are destroyed and people's lives are wrecked. We look back with shame nowadays at what Christians did to Galileo in God's name. And it is very confusing. Very confusing!

Question the beautiful earth, question the beautiful sea,
question the beautiful air, amply spread everywhere. Question
the beautiful sky, question the constellations of stars, question
the sun making the day glorious with its brightness, question
the moon tempering the darkness of the following night with
its splendour . . . They all answer you, 'Take a look! We are
beautiful.' Their beauty is their witness. Who made these
beautiful, changeable things, if not the Great Unchanging
Beauty?

Augustine, Bishop of Hippo, 354–430

But God is a good God. Do not waver in that conviction. 'But people do bad things!' Well of course they do! But even when people are doing bad things, God is a good God. I believe that with all my heart because of (and despite) everything that this life has revealed. God is a good God. Hold onto simple things. Good is better than evil. Light is better than darkness. Love is better than hate. Beauty is better than ugliness. And the Kingdom will come.

> God does not die on the day when we cease to believe in a personal deity, but we die on the day when our lives cease to be illumined by the steady radiance of a wonder, the source of which is beyond all reason.
>
> *Dag Hammarskjöld, first Secretary General of the United Nations, 1905–61*

Lift your eyes and look to the heavens. Refocus your vision on the scale of the project on which God is working. Be patient. Do not despair. Keep hope. For he is all I have, and if I don't have him I have nothing at all. If I don't have him I have no red, wondrous, awe-inspiring, mystical sunrise; I just have the turning of the planet on its axis which diffracts the colours of light through the haphazard weather. 'Do you not know? Have you not heard? Has it not been told you?' God is a good God. And the Kingdom will come.

Detox: Go to the window, night or day, and look up at the cloud, the sun, the stars and beyond. Let what you can see lead you into a sense of amazement about what you can't see. Remind yourself of the scale of the project on which God is working.

God of the cosmos, I am staggered that you are listening to me. For you are you. And I am only I. Thank you.

Day 35

Let God speak

Why is it that when we pray God sometimes seems to be silent? I wonder whether he is speaking as loud as is possible for a human to register, but we don't hear him because our expectations of how to recognize his voice are so limited.

Some years ago I was in Perth, western Australia, where I had been invited to speak at a camp for families at an isolated but spectacular spot in the outback. For someone who likes the comforts of home more than most, it was a bit of an ordeal. It coincided with one of the hottest summers that Australia had endured, and the huts, which were in a forest clearing, had primitive sanitation and no electricity.

Swarthy Australian teenagers would slap me on the back and yell, 'Isn't this beaut, cobber! Bet you haven't got anything like this back in England!'

'No, we haven't,' I replied, forcing my teeth into a smile so that no one could hear me add, 'Thank goodness!'

One night the lads came and asked me, 'Do you wanna come bivvying with us under the stars tonight?' I am not quite sure why they interpreted the way blood drained from my face as a 'yes'. Two hours later, lying under a blanket in the middle of nowhere, I

> Since the creation of the world God's invisible qualities – his eternal power and divine nature – have been clearly seen, being understood from what has been made.
>
> *Romans 1.20*

found myself wondering how I had managed to get myself into such an uncharacteristic situation. I decided that I must have misheard them and thought they had invited me to come bevvying!

Just before dawn one of the guys shook me awake and I sat up with a fright wondering where my bed had gone. He put his finger to his lips and pointed between the trees. A family of kangaroos was standing closer to us than I have ever been to wild animals, except in a zoo. We stood there in silence. A line of half-naked men and a line of suspicious kangaroos face to face as the sun rose red on the horizon. It was a truly sensational sight.

I wondered whether I should try to put into words the awe that we were all feeling in the presence of such a glorious view. But I was beaten. A 13-year-old boy who had been aggressively uninterested in the spiritual parts of the programme whispered, 'It looks like God's been here already.' I thought he was joking, so I smiled and turned my head to join in the joke. But, looking at his face, I saw that he was absolutely serious. I knew I had been standing next to a typical teenager but, with a sudden rush of joy, I realized that I was standing next to a believer.

In the Old Testament we read about the time in the history of the Hebrews when they were led by judges, a succession of heroic men and women who ensured that the people were victorious against their enemies. It was a bloody and chaotic time, and the writer of the book tells us that 'messages from God were rare' (1 Samuel 3.1). One of the last of that line of leaders was the priest Eli who, as a priest with wayward children, must have found himself dismayed that the tribes were in an era of a silent God.

> [Jacob said,] 'Surely the Lord is in this place, and I was not aware of it.'
>
> Genesis 28.16

But God was not silent. He was just trying to speak in a different way from anything that had been thought possible. He bypassed the celebrations in the holy places and bypassed the religious leaders. Instead he gave his message to the people through a little child in the middle of the night. Samuel was a young boy wide awake and confused by what he was hearing. He was so conditioned into the correct ways of behaving that he assumed it was Eli calling him in the darkness, so he went and shook him from his sleep. But – all credit to Eli – the old man realized what was going on. It was God breaking through. Recognizing that Samuel was able to sense the presence of God, he defied usual expectations of what a child could do, and helped the boy to work out what God was communicating.

Do we perhaps miss God's word because we only expect it to come through certain people? Or only in certain places? Might we search for God to speak to us through the Bible when in fact he is trying to speak to us through a newspaper? Do we despair that we do not feel God telling us what his plan is for our work, when he is trying to make it plain through an e-mail from the human resources department? Do we hear nothing that addresses our inmost needs through a preacher, when God is communicating to us loud and clear through a doctor?

> God is like one who, while hiding in a dark room, clears his throat and so gives himself away.
>
> Meister Eckhart, monk, 1260–1327

At the lowest point of his life, Jacob fled his family because he knew that his brother Esau was trying to get revenge for being cheated. His life was in danger, and he was hoping for refuge in a distant country with a relative he had never met. It was an empty, frightening, anonymous time and he was in a desert – actually and metaphorically.

He lay down on a stone pillow. But it was in that completely unpromising place that God broke through to him. He had a vision of being protected and delivered. And when he woke up he named the place Bethel (*Beth-El* means the Gateway to the House of God).

> May none of God's wonderful works keep silence, night or morning. Bright stars, high mountains, the depths of the seas, sources of rushing rivers: may all these break into song as we sing to Father, Son and Holy Spirit. May all the angels in the heavens reply: Amen, Amen, Amen. Power, praise, honour, eternal glory to God, the only giver of grace, Amen, Amen, Amen.
>
> *Anonymous, from the Egyptian desert, circa 280*

If you are serious about listening to God, do not limit him by expecting that he can only speak in a prayer. Because he can speak in a desert. Or in a forest in a foreign land. Or through the kindness of a little boy awake in the night. Or through a kangaroo in the glow of a dawn. Or via an annoying Australian punk who has sniggered rudely all through the sermon. Because those are the moments when a stone pillow becomes the gateway to the house of God.

Detox: Analyse some of the things that you have usually thought of as obstacles to God communicating with you: noisy things, boring things, secular things. Ask God whether he wants you to recognize his message through these as well as through church, prayer and the Bible. Are you seeking his will about something to which you already know the answer?

Lord God, take me by surprise all over again. Let everything that is ordinary speak to me of your presence, your plan and your interest in all the details of my life. Amen.

Day 36

Pray relentlessly

I am a farmer in Bangladesh who ekes out a living on the massive delta that makes up my country. I watch with trepidation as a huge corporation buys up stretches of the coastline in order to farm prawns. The reason I am worried is that I see them clearing the mangrove swamps which have taken a century to grow in order to create the salt lakes that are needed for a tiger prawn farm. And it turns out that I was right to be worried because every four or five years a cyclone hits Bangladesh and floods miles of it. In the natural order of things the rains have been a positive event, replenishing the stocks and nourishing the soil. But that was with the shelter of the mangroves. Now there is no protection from the power of the weather, and the flood comes in not as a blessing, but as a killer that destroys my house and wipes out my crop. So I cry, 'It's so unfair, it's so unfair! I worked so hard for this harvest, and to whom can I go for justice?'

Jesus told the story of a widow who pleaded for justice from a corrupt judge to people who were treated as economic commodities in the vast Roman empire. They knew what it meant to pray desperately to God about a situation in which they were utterly deprived of justice.

In this country we don't often come to God with the same desperation. Sometimes, but not often! We are blessed to live in a country where most people get treated fairly most of the time. So when we pray to God we tend to have different things in mind. I can imagine myself giving a

Jesus told his disciples a parable to show them that they should always pray and not give up. He said: 'In a certain town there was a judge who neither feared God nor cared about people. And there was a widow in that town who kept coming to him with the plea, "Grant me justice against my adversary." For some time he refused. But finally he said to himself, "Even though I don't fear God or care about people, yet because this widow keeps bothering me, I will see that she gets justice, so that she won't eventually wear me out with her coming!"' And the Lord said, 'Listen to what the unjust judge says. And will not God bring about justice for his chosen ones, who cry out to him day and night? Will he keep putting them off? I tell you, he will see that they get justice, and quickly. However, when the Son of Man comes, will he find faith on the earth?'

Luke 18.1–8

dinner party and wanting to serve prawns because I've got a splendid white wine in the fridge. I go to the corner shop and they've sold out. So I go to the local store and they've sold out too. At that stage I am panicking because it's gone six o'clock, so I drive at top speed to the supermarket praying, 'Please God, let them have prawns. Please God, please God!' I'm completely oblivious at that stage to the fact that my appetite for seafood is making farmers in Asia destitute.

When Jesus taught his disciples that they should always pray and not give up, which kind of prayer did he have in mind – more like prawn shoppers or more like prawn farmers? You don't have to be an archbishop to work that out! At the end of his parable Jesus made it clear that he was talking about praying for justice, so that

Be joyful always; pray continually; give thanks in all circumstances, for this is God's will for you in Christ Jesus.

1 Thessalonians 5.16–18

we don't have unrealistic expectations that God will give us whatever self-centred trivial thing we nag him about, because we can't find a parking space, or because it's so important that the opposition misses a penalty, or because we need the teacher to forget to collect the homework we haven't done. No wonder we are sometimes disappointed by the results of our prayers!

So how can you know what you should be praying for, and what just trivializes God's plan for the world? My suggestion is that you pray about absolutely everything, big or small, troubling or trifling, at any time or any place. Obviously there will be some occasions, perhaps many, when God's response is not what we hope for. However, by relentlessly taking every detail of our lives to God, we learn something different. In the persistence with which we pray, we come to know and understand God better and better. As with any friend, lover or colleague with whom we pass time, we come to learn the mind of God. And, remarkably, as we learn his ways, our own wants and aspirations come more and more into line with God's wants and aspirations. He loves justice, so we learn to love justice, which is how we come to pray with understanding for justice, and then we find ourselves working for justice. Over time we find ourselves praying naturally for the things that God desires, and that is when we begin to recognize God answering our prayers, and our own part in those answers.

> I have been driven many times to my knees by the overwhelming conviction that I had nowhere else to go. My own wisdom and that of all about me seemed insufficient for the day.
>
> Abraham Lincoln, President of the USA, 1809–65

For Bangladeshi Christians, 'Come, return Lord Jesus!' is a relentless prayer. 'Return and put right all that is unjust, as you have promised.' And Jesus will. That is the Christian hope. At the right time, Christ will step directly into human affairs to put an end to what is wrong, and to establish a kingdom of endless justice. If the lousy judge in the parable took action, how much more faith we can have that Jesus, our good and gracious Saviour, will return to be the ultimate answer to every prayer that has been uttered?

> Holy Spirit, think through me, until your ideas are my ideas.
>
> *Amy Carmichael, missionary to Asia, 1867–1951*

Here's something strange! In the countries of the prawn buyers, like the UK, the number of people who go to church is dwindling by about a hundred a day. In the countries of the prawn farmers, like Bangladesh, the Church is growing at a phenomenal rate – about ten times the rate at which Christianity is declining in Europe. Where will the Son of Man find faith on earth when he returns? In the places where people who have no one else to turn to, turn to him. In places where they know what it means to throw yourself on the mercy of the Judge of judges, like the persistent widow in the story.

Detox: Buy a newspaper today. Read it with the intention of praying about situations for which you have never prayed before. Lift to God all the places in the world where people are denied justice, trying to see the news reports through his eyes. Then think about whether you might make a habit of expanding the range of places and people for whom you pray.

God of all the world, when I am eager to pray, remind me what really matters; when I am bored with prayer, remind me why it really matters. Amen.

Day 37

Be patient

What a beautiful word 'instant' is! Instant credit, instant entertainment, instant access to anything you could conceivably want to know on the internet. Fantastic! Instant coffee that saves you waiting for it to percolate. Instant money that comes from a machine in the wall and saves you having to queue. Instant meals, heated at the press of a button without the bother of chopping a single vegetable. What a world!

Don't hold me back! I want it all and I want it now. I want the train to roll into the station at the very moment I step onto the platform. I want the pizza delivery boy at my door before I put the phone down. I want Christmas to be tomorrow.

I sometimes think I wasn't really cut out to be a Christian. I want all the benefits of a life-long relationship with God. (But I want them all to come in one weekend.)

I want to learn all that God can teach me. (But please can I have it in the comfort of my own home, instead of going through all those experiences that take me to disaster and

> Be patient, then, brothers and sisters, until the Lord's coming. See how the farmer waits for the land to yield its valuable crop, patiently waiting for the autumn and spring rains. You too, be patient and stand firm, because the Lord's coming is near.
>
> *James 5.7–8*

back, leaving me wondering what God can possibly be up to?)

I want the wisdom that comes from the ups and downs of following God. (But I would rather have it from one easy-on-the-eye DVD that can transform my life in 90 minutes.)

I want the reassurance that God's guidance will lead me towards a good future. (But if he doesn't give it to me by Tuesday it will be quite clear that he doesn't care about me at all.)

Please God, wave a magic wand over me to turn me into a good Christian! Don't tell me that the only way to achieve this will be by learning from my experiences! If you're going to involve me in the interminably slow process of getting me ready for heaven, then I'll be dead before I get there!

When the Bible tells the stories of the great followers of God, it concentrates on the highlights. For example, we hear how the recently-converted Paul dramatically escaped an assassination attempt and fled back to his birthplace, Tarsus. The next we hear of him, he has emerged as someone ready to lead the Church at Antioch. What happened between the two events? We don't know, because it wasn't significant enough to record. But we do know that ten years have gone by.

In Moses' case it took even longer. He was 40 when he left the palace of the Pharaoh in disgrace, having killed a man. He was 80 when he returned to demand the release of the Hebrew people. For four decades he worked as a farmer. No one knows what happened in that time, but God was indisputably at work.

> Those who are patient have great understanding, but the quick-tempered display folly. A heart at peace gives life to the body, but envy rots the bones.
>
> *Proverbs 14.29–30*

Many years before, Jacob had to run away from home because he feared a revenge attack by his wronged brother Esau. He took shelter far away with a relative he had never met. It was 20 years before he met his brother again, but by that time he was transformed into a generous man, ready to be reconciled rather than to fight. God taught him so much in two decades that it turned his life around.

How did Jacob learn so much? It was from the slow haul of life. It wasn't from a sermon or a religious book (in fact, I doubt whether he had any experience of worshipping God during those decades – it wasn't the culture of pagan Paddan Aram). He learnt because he was acutely aware of God involved in his daily life. There were, of course, marvellous moments when he learnt a lot very quickly, like being adopted into a new family, or losing his virginity, or seeing his new-born child. But mostly he learnt through hard, patient graft – work, success, being cheated, being trapped in a loveless marriage, developing business skills.

The fact is, although this 40 day detox will do you the world of good, reading a book is not the way God teaches us the most significant things in our growth as Christians. They come from experiences at which we look back and glimpse God. They come from the blunders that make us realize we are never, never

> The whole point of being alive is the healing of the heart's eye through which God is seen.
>
> Augustine, Bishop of Hippo, 354–430

going to do something again. They come from the successes that convince us that God is a good God who has our best interests at heart. They come from the heartache and the laughter and the slog. Ten years, 20 years, 40 years!

Dramatic revelations of God have their place. Of course they do! Paul encountered Jesus in a vision so bright that he was blinded for three days. Moses' confrontation with God in a burning bush was so frightening that he hid his face. Jacob had an awesome dream of angels that left him convinced he was at the gate of heaven. But in each case, the things that shaped their lives happened in everyday circumstances and mundane places. They went through years with God by their side, God in their thoughts, God opening their eyes to blessings they might not otherwise have seen, God creating new possibilities out of old problems, God consciously woven into the unspectacular business of getting through life as they grew older and wiser and increasingly fulfilled.

And now I feel an admission is being forced out of me! I would almost certainly be a better person if I stopped wanting God to make everything dramatically clear for me before lunchtime, and started looking back over the last 40 marvellous years. Much as my impatient nature hates to admit it, God is imperceptibly making me into a person who is ready to meet him. That is the destiny of us all. I think it's time I started thanking him for the long, slow haul of the journey of discovery we have both been on together.

> Our real blessings often appear to us in the shape of pains, losses and disappointments; but let us have patience, and we soon shall see them in their proper figures.
>
> Joseph Addison, poet, 1672–1719

Detox: Make a list of the three or four most important things you have learnt in life. How did God teach them? Through ordinary or unusual circumstances? Through sermons and books, or through people and places? Painfully or joyfully? Acknowledge to God the value of the journey you and he have been on together.

Unseen God, do to me all that it takes to prepare me for my destiny – to meet you face to face. Amen.

Day 38

Stop trying

My first job was as a teacher. Once, when I was showing two new infants the school, I was impressing upon them the importance of doing what teachers told them straight away. Suddenly I saw an older boy running along the corridor at full tilt and shouted a reprimand: 'Neil!' The two infants immediately knelt down!

I have exaggerated that story so much that the people to whom it happened would scarcely recognize it. The truth is that I was not the sort of teacher who wielded instant authority. When children were naughty I was more tempted to join in than to tell them off! I was never likely to be promoted in a school in which the teachers competed to be the most strict.

I should imagine that Jesus' disciples were involved in that kind of rivalry when he reproached them for wanting to be the greatest. Who knows what the scoring system

[Jesus] asked them, 'What were you arguing about on the road?' But they kept quiet because on the way they had argued about who was the greatest. Sitting down, Jesus called the twelve and said, 'If anyone wants to be first, he must be the very last, and the servant of all.' He took a little child whom he placed among them. Taking the child in his arms, he said to them, 'Whoever welcomes one of these little children in my name welcomes me.'

Mark 9.33–37

was! Perhaps they were debating their pecking order in Jesus' affections, or the number of followers they had won to his cause, or the one who had clocked up the most compassionate acts. I would love to have seen their faces when Jesus chose some urchin, red-handed from a misdemeanour, and picked him out as an example of greatness in the Kingdom of God. Or was it a younger child, rather shy as she found herself the centre of attention? Or maybe a baby, hungry and on the verge of tears in Jesus' arms?

We are inclined to miss the point of what Jesus did because our generation has a different attitude to children. We see this story rather sentimentally. But Jesus chose a child as his example of greatness because in the Jewish culture of the time children were at the bottom of the heap. They were a drain on resources because they had to be fed and clothed long before they were able to contribute to the economic growth of the family. They were, in their earliest years, completely dependent and gave nothing back – except love. Jesus was saying that the state in which we are closest to God is when we are completely dependent and give nothing back – except love.

Jesus was endlessly attracted to people like that – those with socially unacceptable diseases, women with complicated histories of relationships, men with jobs that were not considered of any worth, despised prostitutes. He sought

---

There was a Pharisee named Nicodemus, a member of the Jewish ruling council. He came to Jesus at night and said, 'Rabbi, we know you are a teacher who has come from God. For you could not perform the miraculous signs you are doing if God were not with you.' In reply Jesus declared, 'I tell you the truth, no one can see the kingdom of God without being born again.'

John 3.1–3

---

out the company both of people who were worn down by sinning, and people who were worn down by being sinned against. It must have perplexed those who were successful, religious and good when he told them that on the day they join the queue for the Kingdom of Heaven they would see in front of them people who were weak, agnostic and bad.

Why is uselessness the most important virtue in the Kingdom? Because that is the only way God can accept us. He can't accept us if we present our credentials of good behaviour; they can never be good enough. He can't accept us wearing any kind of medal which says, 'I've repented, I've converted, I've made a commitment.' There are too many 'I's in all those claims. The point at which God accepts us is when we say to him, 'I can't do it. You do it!' And for some Christians – successful, strong, charming people – that is the hardest thing of all.

> Jesus came to raise the dead. The only qualification for the gift of the gospel is to be dead. You don't have to be smart. You don't have to be good. You don't have to be wise. You don't have to be wonderful. You don't have to be anything. You just have to be dead. That's it!
>
> *Robert Farrar Capon, priest and cook, born 1927*

The point at which I was most useful to God was on the first day I was alive – vulnerable, needing constant care, open to anything God wants to do. I've spent 45 years trying to grow out of that. It's not what I did all those A levels for! So, it is incredibly hard for me to hear God say, 'I want you to come to me with all the nothing you had on that first day. I will do everything it takes for you to be mine for all eternity.'

I feel like the religious leader Nicodemus, coming to Jesus with all his achievements and dignity, and asking, 'What is the secret?' And Jesus said to him, 'You must be born once more. Go back to the first moments you were alive, and in that state God will be there for you.' Poor Nicodemus! He must have longed for the day when he would serve as archbishop under Jesus' magnificent reign. It must have utterly broken his heart to lay Jesus in a tomb before his fourth decade was out.

But that is part of the extraordinary grace of God as well. Everything he has done for humankind has sprung from weakness. When he blessed earth with his presence he did it by being born – becoming a helpless infant in Mary's arms. He didn't have to! He could, after all, have arrived on the planet as a warrior resplendent in power, ready to win the world for himself. But instead his achievement was won out of uselessness.

> I am so weak that I can hardly write. I cannot read my Bible. I cannot even pray. I can only lie still in God's arms like a little child, and trust.
>
> James Hudson Taylor, missionary to China, 1832–1905

Jesus didn't have to die. What a useless, ridiculous, almost blasphemous thing to do when the world was so much in need of a Saviour! But out of the weakness of God comes the model for the glory of every human – to exhale our last, weakest breath and then to wake into vivid resurrection.

Hallelujah!

Detox: Lie down on your bed and, in your imagination, work your way backwards through your life. Shed your achievements, your job, your exam results, your knowledge of the Bible and anything else you are proud of. Go back to your earliest memories and picture yourself as a small child. Introduce yourself to Jesus, and find out what he says.

Lord Jesus, I can't. But you can. Amen.

Day 39

Struggle

I sometimes meet Christian people whose experience of life seems to involve them leaping from one burst of power to another. They manage to live every single day as if it is Easter. Or, at least, it seems like that on the surface. With all my heart I wish that my experience was like that. I am very confident indeed that one day in heaven our existence will be unsullied joy. But, to be honest, my life as a Christian has all been a bit of a struggle. I wouldn't swap it for any other, but there has been illness and disappointment along the way, and more occasions on which I've let God down than I care to remember. I've had as many Good Friday lows as Easter Sunday highs.

If you go to church every Sunday, at some point during March or April you will celebrate Palm Sunday, remembering the triumph with which Jesus was welcomed into his capital city. Then, a week later, you will celebrate his resurrection, and thrill to its glorious victory. But there is a danger of missing out the appalling suffering that happened to Jesus in between.

> I want to know Christ and the power of his resurrection and the fellowship of sharing in his sufferings, becoming like him in his death, and so, somehow, to attain to the resurrection from the dead.
>
> *Philippians 3.10–11*

The church calendar was designed in the days when

Christians went to church every day between Palm Sunday and Easter Sunday. Five centuries ago, congregations would have dwelt at length on the desperate sadness of Jesus' farewell to his disciples, his arrest, his suffering and his despicable execution. That was a very profound spiritual journey to undertake in a week. In fact, there was a strong incentive to make that journey, because in Elizabethan England people were fined for not attending church. The fine was one shilling for each of the seven days that you didn't show up. Given that 12 pence bought nine gallons of milk, the fine was the equivalent of about £20.

Today, when 12 pence doesn't even buy a pint of semi-skimmed, Good Friday is almost indistinguishable from any other day. That makes it even more important that, during this detox, we put aside time to acknowledge the struggle that it takes to follow the way of Jesus. In the gospel of untroubled success all our prayers are answered, all our illnesses are healed, all our hopes are fulfilled, and every day is the springtime of resurrection. But life is not like that. Worship that has no struggle in it rushes past Good Friday to reach Easter Sunday, and leaves us with no resources to deal with disappointments when they come, as they inevitably will.

When Paul wrote to the church at Philippi about what he most wanted in life, the things he chose were unexpected.

I remember my affliction and my wandering, the bitterness and the gall. I well remember them, and my soul is downcast within me. Yet this I call to mind and therefore I have hope: Because of the Lord's great love we are not consumed, for his compassions never fail. They are new every morning; great is your faithfulness. I say to myself, 'The Lord is my portion; therefore I will wait for him.'

Lamentations 3.19–25

He explained that he wanted 'the power of Christ's resurrection'. That's not surprising at all. However, he also wrote that he wanted 'the fellowship of sharing in his sufferings'. Now that is shocking! It is not a gospel of untroubled success at all. So in what way is there power in the struggle as well as in the triumph?

There is a power in knowing Jesus that is rooted in the past. It is powerful because it is objective. The things Jesus did, and the person he was, stand unchangeable in history. They don't depend on how you are feeling, or what the mood of society is, or the spirit of the age. No one is ever going to undo what God has done through Jesus in space and time on our own planet. There is no better way to fill your detox with meaning than to read the story of what Jesus did and said. The power comes from knowing that you are not taking the values of your life from someone's hand-me-down version of faith, but from the Jesus whom you have encountered in the pages of the Bible.

There is a power in knowing the resurrection

> What kind of man is this who for our sakes is hanging on the cross, whose suffering causes the rocks themselves to crack and crumble with compassion, whose death brings the dead back to life? Let my heart crack and crumble at the sight of him. Let my soul break apart with compassion for his suffering. Let it be shattered with grief at my sins for which he dies. And finally let it be softened with devoted love for him.
>
> *Bonaventura, theologian, 1221–74*

that is rooted in the future. There will never be a point in your Christian life when you will have no hope left. Why? Because we have a God who knows the way out of a grave. When you have put your faith in something more powerful than death itself, what is there left to imprison you?

But there is also a power that is absolutely rooted in the present, and it is the power of struggling alongside Jesus. Of course, there is nothing glamorous about hardship, doubt or pain. Even Good Friday has the wrong name. In the days when milk cost 12 pence for nine gallons it was known as God Friday, and the name has changed over the centuries.

But those who walk the path of Christ will at some stages of their life walk through a kind of Calvary. And the needy people of the world can only hear voices that come from Calvary. Being successful is not always useful when it comes to serving God. Genuinely valuable service involves being able to stand beside people in shared failure, to stumble together in shared weakness, to pray side by side in shared uncertainty. That is the fellowship of sharing in Jesus' sufferings about which Paul wrote. It's a struggle. But it's a powerful struggle. And we need to go through it if the joy of resurrection is going to have its full meaning.

> Since the communion of last Easter I have led a life so dissipated and useless, and my terrors and perplexities have so much increased, that I am under great depression and discouragement; yet I purpose to present myself before God tomorrow, with humble hope that he will not break the bruised reed.
>
> *Samuel Johnson, writer, 1709–84*

Detox: Read the account of the last days of Jesus' life from one of the Gospels. As you do, pretend that you don't know how the story ends. Experience the sadness, and recognize that Jesus is one who has shared with you all the difficulty that human life can bring. Remind yourself that whatever struggle may be still to come, it is a route along which Jesus himself has already trodden.

Lord Jesus, it is useless to ask for a life without suffering, and absurd to ask for a life with suffering. So give me neither. Instead give me the patience, insight and power that comes from recognizing you alongside me in the struggle. Amen.

Day 40

Praise

What a glorious thing it is to waste time! What a joy! Setting out on a daft conversation with a friend at eleven o'clock at night, knowing that it will wind its way into the early hours and in the morning you will have nothing to show for it. Glorious!

Lighting a hundred candles because someone is coming to dinner, and spending an entire day looking forward to it because the romance of it is irresistible. Splendid!

Getting stuck into a book, with the pages turning and turning, and not wanting to stop even though you know you'll have to wear an unironed shirt in the morning. Marvellous!

Praise God in his sanctuary;
praise him in his mighty heavens.
Praise him for his acts of power;
praise him for his surpassing greatness.
Praise him with the sounding of the trumpet,
praise him with the harp and lyre,
praise him with tambourine and dancing,
praise him with the strings and flute,
praise him with the clash of cymbals,
praise him with resounding cymbals.
Let everything that has breath praise the Lord.

Psalm 150.1–6

Deciding that, although there are 20 reasons why you shouldn't, what you really want to do is take the family to the zoo. 'Blow the tax returns, take me to the tigers!' Catastrophic as far as work is concerned, but what fun!

I've done all four of those things in the last few months, and what a waste of time it's been. I wish there had been more! At the zoo I told my god-daughter she is gorgeous, which is indisputable! At the end of the book I texted the friend who recommended it to say that she has the best artistic taste in London, which is true. With a hundred candles alight I told my best friends that I value them more than anything else in life, which is correct. And in the early hours of the morning I told young Paul that letting him come and live in the guest room is the best thing I have ever done, which is . . . pushing it a bit!

I suppose it is all praise really. I say those words to my god-daughter because I want her to grow up knowing she is valued. I want my literary friend to feel glad that she is capable of making someone's life richer. I want my friends to realize that my life has been happy simply for having had them as part of it for 20 years. And I want Paul to pay his phone bill!

They already knew those things. I didn't need to tell them again. My relationship with them all would be just as good without the zoo, the candles, the texting or the wide-awake night. I don't really know why I did any of them. Those people won't love me any more or any less. I just wanted to waste time with them because if there is nothing to praise and love and value and enjoy, what's the point of a relationship?

Psalm 150 finds the songwriter wasting time with God in praise and love and value and enjoyment. Is there any point to it all? No, of course not! Does God need to be told he is powerful, great or holy? Obviously not – he knows perfectly well already. Are we going to get preferential treatment from him if we say the right words? Not a chance! The fact that there is no point to it means that it is during the times when we are praising God that the real measure of our relationship with him is evident, for better or for worse.

> But you are a chosen people, a royal priesthood, a holy nation, a people belonging to God, that you may declare the praises of him who called you out of darkness into his wonderful light.
>
> *1 Peter 2.9*

Maybe we are using the empty words of a relationship in which communication has stopped. Or perhaps we are using the embarrassing, over-the-top words of a love letter in smudged ink, which we know will be pored over for every shade of their meaning. Or maybe these are words spoken through gritted teeth because it's so important to keep the relationship going, but it's hard work because of disappointment, or hurt, or just the boredom of having done it for so long. Or are they the words you find when rifling through a poetry book for something to say to a friend when you know that your own words would be inadequate? Or it is possible that we have reached the moment when words come to an end between two people so at ease with each other that they just relax silently in each other's presence?

> Be not lax in celebrating. Be not lazy in the festive praise of God. Be ablaze with enthusiasm. Let us be an alive, burning offering before the altar of God.
>
> *Hildegard of Bingen, nun and composer, 1098–1179*

You couldn't give an explanation of praise to someone who doesn't believe – it's *such* a great waste of time. You wouldn't need an explanation of praise to someone who does believe – it's such a *great* waste of time.

At this very moment, every living creature that God has

made is praising him. And every inert thing praises him just by existing. The seeds praise him in their sprouting. The birds praise him in their flight. The sea praises him in its ebb and flow. The viruses praise him in their multiplying. The mountains praise him in their towering. The rain praises him in its wetness. The oxygen praises him in its life-giving. The planets praise him in their orbiting. Every created thing praises God by doing spontaneously what he put it there to do. When humans praise God we are simply joining the cosmos to do what comes naturally: to express how good God is. How holy, how wonderful, how powerful, how God!

But there is one difference with humans. Of all the things created with the potential to praise God, they are the one element which has the choice not to. That is the risk God took. It's the risk any lover takes. God made himself vulnerable to people deciding not to bother. To decide that wasting away time with God is a waste of time.

Let's not make that mistake! Let's join everything in creation to praise the Lord! Let's crazily decide at eleven o'clock at night to stay up chatting! Let's light a hundred candles! Let's get stuck into a book of the Bible for page after page and leave all the clothes unironed! Let's stupidly decide on a day out at the zoo, or any place where 'everything that has breath' will be praising God alongside us! In music or in silence, in church or in solitude, let's learn from the relationships we have with those whom we love how to keep alive our relationship with the one who loved us first and best.

> Arise, my soul, arise! It is good to rejoice and join the angels' praises, for it is our health and strength.
>
> *Elizabeth of Schönau, nun, 1129–64*

Detox: Today of all days, surely you don't need me to tell you what to do! Tell God, at the end of this detox, just how you are!

God, who is the Lord of each atom of creation, every single thing you have made is agog with praise at this moment, and so, quietly and humbly, I would like to add my voice to theirs. Amen.